JUMBLE® Safari

IN SEARCH OF UNDISCOVERED PUZZLES!

Jeff Knurek
and
Mike Argirion

TRIUMPH
BOOKS

This book is available in quantity at special discounts
for your group or organization.

For further information, contact:

Triumph Books LLC
542 South Dearborn Street
Suite 750
Chicago, Illinois 60605
(312) 939-3330
Fax (312) 663-3557
www.triumphbooks.com

Printed in U.S.A.

ISBN: 978-1-60078-675-4

Design by Sue Knopf

CONTENTS

Classic Puzzles

Daily Puzzles

Challenger Puzzles

Answers

JUMBLE®

SAFARI

Classic Puzzles

JUMBLE®

Unscramble these four Jumbles, one letter to each square, to form four ordinary words.

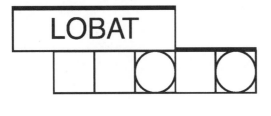

LOBAT

GALEE

THEVIR

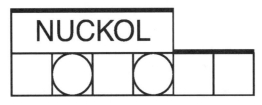

NUCKOL

I do the cooking, cleaning, laundry and...

Well, I take out the garbage

WHEN THE DENTIST AND HIS MANICURIST WIFE FOUGHT, IT WAS----

Now arrange the circled letters to form the surprise answer, as suggested by the above cartoon.

AND

JUMBLE®

Unscramble these four Jumbles, one letter to
each square, to form four ordinary words.

HICCK

TOAQU

MAZECE

COMEEB

I'll do better next time

WHAT THE
BOOMERANG
CHAMPION SOUGHT
WHEN HE LOST
THE CONTEST.

Now arrange the circled letters to form the
surprise answer, as suggested by the above
cartoon.

Print answer here A " ⬡⬡⬡⬡⬡⬡⬡⬡ "

JUMBLE®

Unscramble these four Jumbles, one letter to each square, to form four ordinary words.

GUBOS

FLECT

MIULEH

CHYSIP

Berg straight ahead!

WHAT IT TAKES TO SPOT A DISTANT ICE SITE.

Now arrange the circled letters to form the surprise answer, as suggested by the above cartoon.

Print answer here

JUMBLE®

Unscramble these four Jumbles, one letter to
each square, to form four ordinary words.

GEFUD

MYKUR

NIWWON

REYJES

I'm so happy.
Can I have the
keys, Mom?

THE FIRST THING
THE TEEN TOOK
WHEN HE GOT HIS
DRIVER'S LICENSE.

Now arrange the circled letters to form the
surprise answer, as suggested by the above
cartoon.

Print answer here A " ◯◯◯ " ◯◯◯◯

JUMBLE®

Unscramble these four Jumbles, one letter to each square, to form four ordinary words.

TULIB

TARAL

HERNUT

DORVOE

Now we won't have to drag everything

WHEN THE WHEEL WAS INVENTED, IT CREATED A---

Now arrange the circled letters to form the surprise answer, as suggested by the above cartoon.

Print answer here

JUMBLE®

Unscramble these four Jumbles, one letter to each square, to form four ordinary words.

DIMIO

TAUID

GYSSAR

THERTE

It's supposed to go into the pail

WHEN THE CITY SLICKER TRIED MILKING A COW, THE RESULT WAS----

Now arrange the circled letters to form the surprise answer, as suggested by the above cartoon.

Print answer AN *here* "　　　　　"

JUMBLE®

Unscramble these four Jumbles, one letter to each square, to form four ordinary words.

LAWRD

RIGAN

ROYLOP

WHYROT

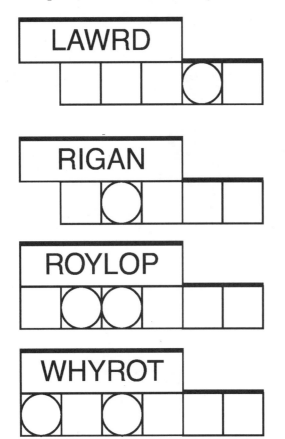

Hey, those are my seats!

Sez who?

A TICKETS MIX-UP CAN RESULT IN A----

Now arrange the circled letters to form the surprise answer, as suggested by the above cartoon.

Print answer here

JUMBLE®

Unscramble these four Jumbles, one letter to each square, to form four ordinary words.

SNUKK

WREEF

FUMINF

RETTUL

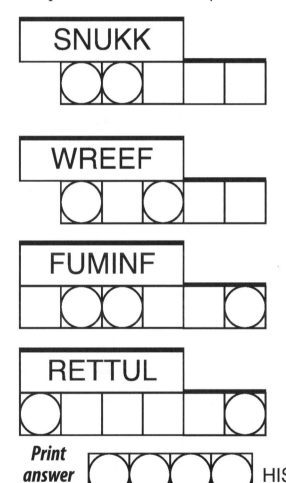

HE WAS NAMED TAXIDERMIST OF THE YEAR BECAUSE HE----

Now arrange the circled letters to form the surprise answer, as suggested by the above cartoon.

Print answer here

 HIS " "

JUMBLE®

Unscramble these four Jumbles, one letter to each square, to form four ordinary words.

YONIS

DAAHE

NUPWOT

RAZABA

Try the meatball recipe. It's my favorite

BOOK SIGNING TODAY!

WHAT A COOKBOOK AUTHOR WILL DO.

Now arrange the circled letters to form the surprise answer, as suggested by the above cartoon.

Print answer here ◯◯◯ HIS ◯◯◯◯◯

JUMBLE®

Unscramble these four Jumbles, one letter to each square, to form four ordinary words.

YILCI

RABDN

TANUBE

FLUFEM

Fill out the forms. It will cost around $50

WHAT IT TAKES TO SHIP A PACKAGE CROSS COUNTRY.

Now arrange the circled letters to form the surprise answer, as suggested by the above cartoon.

Print answer here   A "◯◯◯◯◯◯"

JUMBLE®

Unscramble these four Jumbles, one letter to each square, to form four ordinary words.

ZAMIE

NAHCT

TARDIO

INTIEF

...and my fee is deductible

WHAT HE PAID WHEN HE HIRED THE TAX ADVISOR.

Now arrange the circled letters to form the surprise answer, as suggested by the above cartoon.

Print answer here

JUMBLE®

Unscramble these four Jumbles, one letter to each square, to form four ordinary words.

UNOMT

SNAIE

MOSHNA

DEGUMS

Perfect.
Worth every penny

WHAT THE MALE
MODEL RECEIVED
WHEN HE POSED
IN THE SUIT.

Now arrange the circled letters to form the surprise answer, as suggested by the above cartoon.

Print answer here A " ◯◯◯◯◯◯◯◯◯ " ◯◯◯

JUMBLE®

Unscramble these four Jumbles, one letter to each square, to form four ordinary words.

BUTIC

NARCK

GURCOH

GOAFER

I always wanted a convertible and I got a good deal

WHAT HE DROVE WHEN HE BOUGHT A USED CAR.

Now arrange the circled letters to form the surprise answer, as suggested by the above cartoon.

Print answer here A

JUMBLE®

Unscramble these four Jumbles, one letter to each square, to form four ordinary words.

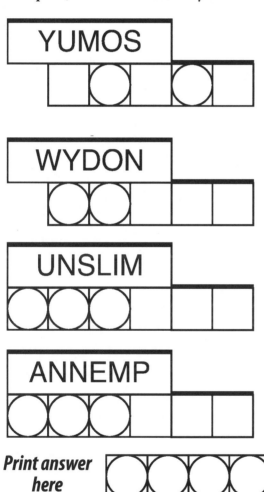

YUMOS

WYDON

UNSLIM

ANNEMP

It'll cost you a pretty pence but I get results

TRAINER

WHAT IT COST THE LONDON MOGUL TO LOSE SOME POUNDS.

Now arrange the circled letters to form the surprise answer, as suggested by the above cartoon.

Print answer here

JUMBLE®

Unscramble these four Jumbles, one letter to each square, to form four ordinary words.

GUVEA

DYPET

UNRICH

VARMEL

Look at him go

WHAT THE SURGEON TURNED INTO AT THE ANNUAL PARTY.

Now arrange the circled letters to form the surprise answer, as suggested by the above cartoon.

Print answer here

A

JUMBLE®

Unscramble these four Jumbles, one letter to each square, to form four ordinary words.

FALEY

HINKT

HERITH

SPRAYT

$10,000!
That's twice the estimate.
I'm not paying

WHAT HAPPENED WHEN HE GOT THE BILL FOR THE ROOF?

Now arrange the circled letters to form the surprise answer, as suggested by the above cartoon.

Print answer here   HE ◯◯◯ THE " ◯◯◯◯◯◯◯ "

JUMBLE®

Unscramble these four Jumbles, one letter to each square, to form four ordinary words.

RIMEN

BYGAG

TRAUGI

DEPHUL

More wattage and less cost

WHAT THE COUPLE GOT IN THE LIGHTING STORE.

Now arrange the circled letters to form the surprise answer, as suggested by the above cartoon.

Print answer here   A   "⬡⬡⬡⬡⬡⬡"   ⬡⬡⬡⬡

JUMBLE®

Unscramble these four Jumbles, one letter to
each square, to form four ordinary words.

CIMEN

LASIA

BLIMEN

SYTHAN

THE WORKERS
DESCRIBED THE
NASTY TYCOON
AS---

Now arrange the circled letters to form the
surprise answer, as suggested by the above
cartoon.

Print answer
here   A ⃝⃝⃝ OF " ⃝⃝⃝⃝⃝ "

19

JUMBLE®

Unscramble these four Jumbles, one letter to each square, to form four ordinary words.

LYKIS

ORFUR

CLUTOC

DRAPEA

The winner gets the big money

WHAT A BOXER WILL FIGHT FOR THAT A WOMAN HAS.

Now arrange the circled letters to form the surprise answer, as suggested by the above cartoon.

Print answer here A ◯◯◯◯◯

JUMBLE®

Unscramble these four Jumbles, one letter to each square, to form four ordinary words.

POCUE

DREEL

AXNYRL

EXDULE

Drinks are on me

He wins again

WHAT THE JANITOR DID WHEN HE PLAYED POKER.

Now arrange the circled letters to form the surprise answer, as suggested by the above cartoon.

Print answer here HE " ◯◯◯◯◯◯◯ " ◯◯

JUMBLE®

Unscramble these four Jumbles, one letter to
each square, to form four ordinary words.

ILVIC

RECEL

TAEGOE

PACALA

You must've
liked the food

WHEN THE SKINNY
LITTLE CONVICT
GAINED WEIGHT IN
PRISON, HE WAS---

Now arrange the circled letters to form the
surprise answer, as suggested by the above
cartoon.

Print answer here " "

JUMBLE®

Unscramble these four Jumbles, one letter to each square, to form four ordinary words.

AMELY

BIBAR

LOUBED

RICHEP

Get the dogs and set up roadblocks

WHAT THE WARDEN DID WHEN THE CROOKED BARBER ESCAPED.

Now arrange the circled letters to form the surprise answer, as suggested by the above cartoon.

Print answer here "  " THE

JUMBLE®

Unscramble these four Jumbles, one letter to each square, to form four ordinary words.

UNGED

ELBIG

RIDOLF

REDDEG

He's always hoeing or weeding

WHAT THE VIOLINIST ENJOYED DOING IN THE GARDEN.

Now arrange the circled letters to form the surprise answer, as suggested by the above cartoon.

Print answer here " ◯◯◯◯◯◯◯◯ "

JUMBLE®

Unscramble these four Jumbles, one letter to each square, to form four ordinary words.

TURET

BUAQS

IMSURT

DUNCIE

Ugh! I can hardly lift this

5-13

WHEN THE COOK DRAINED THE HUGE POT OF PASTA, IT WAS---

Now arrange the circled letters to form the surprise answer, as suggested by the above cartoon.

Print answer here A "〇〇〇〇〇〇"

25

JUMBLE®

Unscramble these four Jumbles, one letter to
each square, to form four ordinary words.

EVVER

IRRAB

TINVER

RUSSED

Where are
you going?

I've got to write
this down

WHEN THE ASPIRING
POET GOT AN IDEA
DURING THE NIGHT,
HE WENT FROM----

Now arrange the circled letters to form the
surprise answer, as suggested by the above
cartoon.

Print answer here ◯◯◯ TO ◯◯◯◯◯◯

JUMBLE®

SAFARI

Daily
Puzzles

JUMBLE®

Unscramble these four Jumbles, one letter to
each square, to form four ordinary words.

RUGPO

SINBO

FOYFAL

UNTEAR

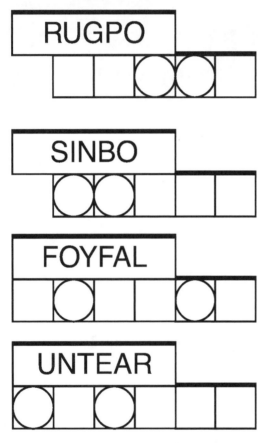

NOW SHOWING

GET OUT OF
THE WATER AGAIN!

Two please

$4.75

5/20

WHEN THEY WENT
TO THE SHARK
MOVIE, IT WAS---

Now arrange the circled letters to form the
surprise answer, as suggested by the above
cartoon.

**Print answer
here**

⬡⬡⬡⬡⬡ A " ⬡⬡⬡ "

JUMBLE.

Unscramble these four Jumbles, one letter to
each square, to form four ordinary words.

DRATY

ZABLE

WHARRO

YADLAM

What's in my future?

I love doing this

WHEN THE SEER
READ THEIR
FORTUNE, SHE---

Now arrange the circled letters to form the
surprise answer, as suggested by the above
cartoon.

Print answer here ◯◯◯ A " ◯◯◯◯ "

JUMBLE®

Unscramble these four Jumbles, one letter to each square, to form four ordinary words.

RYCED

NUCEL

TAMLED

UNBREM

Oh, she's lovely

Such poise

5/24

A BEAUTY QUEEN WILL MAKE HER ENTRANCE TO---

Now arrange the circled letters to form the surprise answer, as suggested by the above cartoon.

Print answer here

JUMBLE®

Unscramble these four Jumbles, one letter to each square, to form four ordinary words.

YAASS

GUSET

LADDEY

RACCIT

Oh! I just had it done

WHEN THE RAIN RUINED HER HAIRDO, SHE WAS ---

Now arrange the circled letters to form the surprise answer, as suggested by the above cartoon.

Print answer here " ☐☐☐-☐☐☐☐☐☐☐ "

JUMBLE®

Unscramble these four Jumbles, one letter to each square, to form four ordinary words.

STURY

PEROW

MAYGIB

PLECOM

Now what do we do?

Where are the oars?

5/29

WHEN THE RUNABOUT STALLED, IT TURNED INTO A ---

Now arrange the circled letters to form the surprise answer, as suggested by the above cartoon.

Print answer here A " ☐☐☐ " ☐☐☐☐☐

JUMBLE®

Unscramble these four Jumbles, one letter to each square, to form four ordinary words.

IMPER

FARCT

SPICET

TUITOW

My husband is so interesting

SHE MARRIED A NOVELIST BECAUSE HE WAS ---

Now arrange the circled letters to form the surprise answer, as suggested by the above cartoon.

Print answer here

"   "

JUMBLE®

Unscramble these four Jumbles, one letter to each square, to form four ordinary words.

GWOIN

GLUID

NOPPIL

MOONIK

She's a fine spotter

Look, it's a ...

THE BLUE-EYED BLONDE LED THE BIRD WATCHERS BECAUSE SHE WAS ----

Now arrange the circled letters to form the surprise answer, as suggested by the above cartoon.

Print answer here " "

JUMBLE®

Unscramble these four Jumbles, one letter to
each square, to form four ordinary words.

SEPIO

EUQUE

BRYDOW

DAVRIE

I've always
dreamed of a
big wedding

THIS CAN RUIN
A RELATIONSHIP

Now arrange the circled letters to form the
surprise answer, as suggested by the above
cartoon.

**Print
answer
here**

" ◯◯◯◯◯ " ◯◯◯◯◯

JUMBLE®

Unscramble these four Jumbles, one letter to each square, to form four ordinary words.

HOCKE

UNGLE

ROTHAX

UNNOIB

Where did she go?

WHEN THE MAGICIAN MADE HIS BEAUTIFUL HELPER DISAPPEAR, SHE WAS ---

Now arrange the circled letters to form the surprise answer, as suggested by the above cartoon.

Print answer here

TO ☐☐☐☐ AT

JUMBLE®

Unscramble these four Jumbles, one letter to each square, to form four ordinary words.

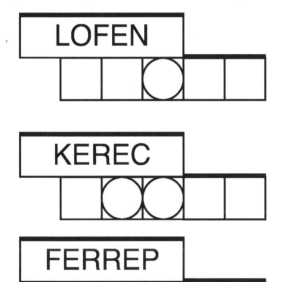

LOFEN

KEREC

FERREP

NAUVEE

BOOM!

BANG!

Oh, relax

Too much noise!

WHAT THE FEUDING NEIGHBORS HAD ON THE FOURTH OF JULY

Now arrange the circled letters to form the surprise answer, as suggested by the above cartoon.

Print answer here   A   "⬡⬡⬡⬡⬡" ⬡⬡

JUMBLE®

Unscramble these four Jumbles, one letter to
each square, to form four ordinary words.

TANCE

TUFLE

BOYDEM

LOWHYL

He doesn't waste
any time

WHEN THE OLD-TIME
TELEGRAPH
OPERATOR SENT HIS
HOURLY MESSAGE,
IT WAS ---

Now arrange the circled letters to form the
surprise answer, as suggested by the above
cartoon.

Print answer here ON  "  "

JUMBLE®

Unscramble these four Jumbles, one letter to each square, to form four ordinary words.

POASY

PHULS

DUPLED

ZARBLE

This will keep us out of the sun

$5.00 an hour

ACCEPTABLE WHEN RENTING A BEACH UMBRELLA

Now arrange the circled letters to form the surprise answer, as suggested by the above cartoon.

Print answer here   " ⬡⬡⬡⬡⬡ " ⬡⬡⬡⬡

JUMBLE®

Unscramble these four Jumbles, one letter to each square, to form four ordinary words.

PLONY

VENIG

FLUNIX

WINDOS

You're hired. Cover that up

DONE BY A LABORER WHEN HE GETS THE JOB

Now arrange the circled letters to form the surprise answer, as suggested by the above cartoon.

Print answer here

⬡⬡⬡⬡⬡ THE " ⬡⬡⬡⬡⬡⬡⬡ "

JUMBLE®

Unscramble these four Jumbles, one letter to each square, to form four ordinary words.

CHUGO

LOCCI

TADWYR

VAHLIS

That's all I've got. Keep the clip.

WHAT THE TYCOON RESORTED TO WHEN HIS ASSETS WERE FROZEN

Now arrange the circled letters to form the surprise answer, as suggested by the above cartoon.

Print answer here

JUMBLE

Unscramble these four Jumbles, one letter to each square, to form four ordinary words.

TELLU

FARCS

ORSOUP

AHNRAG

Get whatever you want

WHAT SHE GOT WHEN THE SUGAR DADDY GAVE HER HIS CREDIT CARD

Now arrange the circled letters to form the surprise answer, as suggested by the above cartoon.

Print answer here A " ◯◯◯◯◯◯◯ " ◯◯◯ ◯◯ IT

JUMBLE®

Unscramble these four Jumbles, one letter to each square, to form four ordinary words.

NORCO

YACKT

RAFIAN

LARBUT

Good mileage, 5-year warranty and ...

Can we afford it?

THIS TAKES SOME STUDY BEFORE A BIG PURCHASE

Now arrange the circled letters to form the surprise answer, as suggested by the above cartoon.

Print answer here A

JUMBLE®

Unscramble these four Jumbles, one letter to each square, to form four ordinary words.

AVUME

NEMOD

TEENIC

WHAIGE

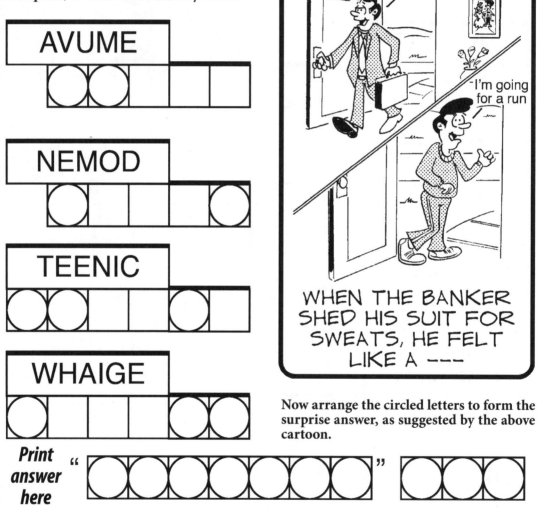

Honey, I'm home

I'm going for a run

WHEN THE BANKER SHED HIS SUIT FOR SWEATS, HE FELT LIKE A ---

Now arrange the circled letters to form the surprise answer, as suggested by the above cartoon.

Print answer here " ⬡⬡⬡⬡⬡⬡⬡ " ⬡⬡⬡

JUMBLE®

Unscramble these four Jumbles, one letter to each square, to form four ordinary words.

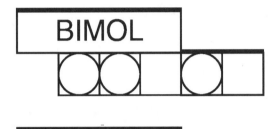

BIMOL

HELEW

DIPSUT

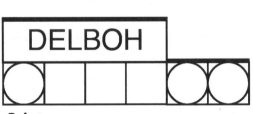

DELBOH

Perfect. Nice job

Here's the final total

WHEN THEIR HOUSE WAS COMPLETED, THE COUPLE WAS ---

Now arrange the circled letters to form the surprise answer, as suggested by the above cartoon.

Print answer here

45

JUMBLE®

Unscramble these four Jumbles, one letter to
each square, to form four ordinary words.

WHASA

VEYHA

MOONID

NERVAG

This may help
someone live

GIVE
BLOOD

A DEPOSIT AT THE
BLOOD BANK
IS A ---

Now arrange the circled letters to form the
surprise answer, as suggested by the above
cartoon.

**Print
answer
here**

 TO " "

JUMBLE®

Unscramble these four Jumbles, one letter to
each square, to form four ordinary words.

PITED

PRUSN

DANCEN

HOGUNE

Here's my bill

Wonderful.
I've lost another
ten

WHAT THE DIETITIAN
DID WHEN THE
ENGLISH PATIENT
LOST WEIGHT

Now arrange the circled letters to form the
surprise answer, as suggested by the above
cartoon.

Print
answer
here

"   "

JUMBLE®

Unscramble these four Jumbles, one letter to each square, to form four ordinary words.

NOAPI

LIGUT

INCANE

SYMFLE

How 'bout another, ol' pal?

Don't mind if I do

THIS CAN MAKE FOR A "GENIAL" EVENING

Now arrange the circled letters to form the surprise answer, as suggested by the above cartoon.

Print answer here ⟨◯◯◯⟩ AND ⟨◯◯◯⟩

JUMBLE®

Unscramble these four Jumbles, one letter to each square, to form four ordinary words.

HORAB

MUBIE

LAROSI

TENJIC

You need to look your best today

THE GROOMER BRUSHED THE SHOW HORSE'S HAIR BECAUSE IT WAS ---

Now arrange the circled letters to form the surprise answer, as suggested by the above cartoon.

Print answer here

" "

JUMBLE®

Unscramble these four Jumbles, one letter to
each square, to form four ordinary words.

ADNUT

ECHLE

BOWELL

DARFOE

I've gained another
five pounds

TOO MANY SQUARE
MEALS CAN MAKE
ONE ---

Now arrange the circled letters to form the
surprise answer, as suggested by the above
cartoon.

Print
answer
here

" "

JUMBLE®

Unscramble these four Jumbles, one letter to each square, to form four ordinary words.

HOACC

FREVE

SEPORC

TERLIP

Come with me, cowboy

SALOON

WHAT THE SHERIFF ALWAYS HAS IN A WESTERN MOVIE.

Now arrange the circled letters to form the surprise answer, as suggested by the above cartoon.

Print answer here   A " ◯◯◯◯ " ◯◯◯◯

JUMBLE®

Unscramble these four Jumbles, one letter to each square, to form four ordinary words.

EBELL

IXAMM

DICLAP

VITANY

Beats me

Royal Flush!

EVEN A KING TAKES A BACK SEAT TO THIS IN A POKER GAME.

Now arrange the circled letters to form the surprise answer, as suggested by the above cartoon.

Print answer here

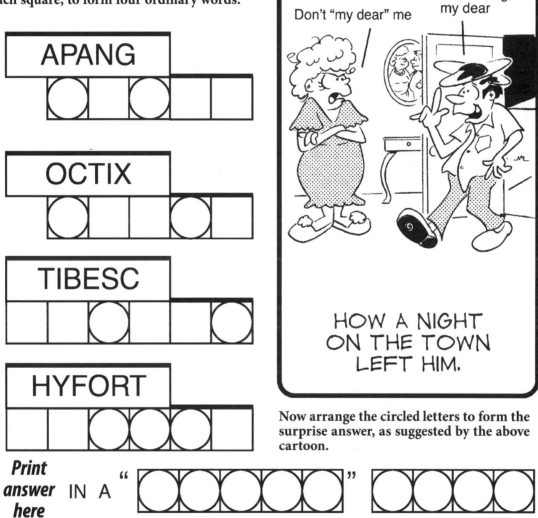

JUMBLE®

Unscramble these four Jumbles, one letter to each square, to form four ordinary words.

APANG

OCTIX

TIBESC

HYFORT

Don't "my dear" me

Good evening, my dear

HOW A NIGHT ON THE TOWN LEFT HIM.

Now arrange the circled letters to form the surprise answer, as suggested by the above cartoon.

Print answer here IN A " ⎔⎔⎔⎔⎔ " ⎔⎔⎔⎔

53

JUMBLE®

Unscramble these four Jumbles, one letter to each square, to form four ordinary words.

YOPPP

OPSOW

TOATER

GLINTE

C'mon! Get with it

WHAT A PHOTO-GRAPHER CAN DO WITH A BORED MODEL.

Now arrange the circled letters to form the surprise answer, as suggested by the above cartoon.

Print answer here

" "

JUMBLE®

Unscramble these four Jumbles, one letter to each square, to form four ordinary words.

SIONE

SNAPY

MYSLOB

LETTEK

First we work on posture, then on rhythm, then...

WHAT IT TAKES TO BECOME A BALLROOM DANCER.

Now arrange the circled letters to form the surprise answer, as suggested by the above cartoon.

Print answer here

◯◯◯◯◯ OF " ◯◯◯◯◯◯ "

JUMBLE®

Unscramble these four Jumbles, one letter to each square, to form four ordinary words.

MYLAN

ALLEG

RILIXE

EXCOBI

STEE-RIKE

Of all the dumb...
Are you blind?

WHEN THE MANAGER
LET OFF STEAM,
HE WAS ---

Now arrange the circled letters to form the surprise answer, as suggested by the above cartoon.

Print answer here "⬡⬡⬡⬡⬡⬡⬡"

JUMBLE®

Unscramble these four Jumbles, one letter to
each square, to form four ordinary words.

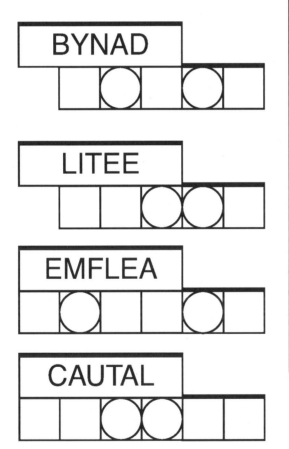

BYNAD

LITEE

EMFLEA

CAUTAL

Has it ever
snowed here?

IT DOESN'T EXIST
AT THE EQUATOR.

Now arrange the circled letters to form the
surprise answer, as suggested by the above
cartoon.

Print answer here

JUMBLE®

Unscramble these four Jumbles, one letter to each square, to form four ordinary words.

PETIR

ZAGUE

PHESCY

MEECHS

Next watch in two hours

Wake me—

WHAT THE GUARD WAS BETWEEN WHEN HE TOOK A REST.

Now arrange the circled letters to form the surprise answer, as suggested by the above cartoon.

Print answer here   THE

JUMBLE®

Unscramble these four Jumbles, one letter to each square, to form four ordinary words.

NOWRC

PARAT

INSENG

TEACKS

He's a Taurus.
She's a Leo

THE HOLLYWOOD
ASTROLOGER LIKED
TO GOSSIP BECAUSE
SHE ---

Now arrange the circled letters to form the surprise answer, as suggested by the above cartoon.

Print answer here THE " "

JUMBLE®

Unscramble these four Jumbles, one letter to each square, to form four ordinary words.

ROMNI

UNFYN

BECKED

REPJUM

Let's do it now

JUSTICE OF THE PEACE

WHAT THE SOLDIERS DID WHEN THEY DECIDED TO GET MARRIED.

Now arrange the circled letters to form the surprise answer, as suggested by the above cartoon.

Print answer here " ◯◯◯◯◯◯◯ " ◯◯

JUMBLE®

Unscramble these four Jumbles, one letter to each square, to form four ordinary words.

WODDY

DEHIC

LENZOZ

GALENT

There's grass to cut, weeds to be pulled...

I need some lemonade

WHEN MOM SCOLDED HIM FOR BEING LAZY, DAD TOOK IT ---

Now arrange the circled letters to form the surprise answer, as suggested by the above cartoon.

Print answer here

JUMBLE®

Unscramble these four Jumbles, one letter to
each square, to form four ordinary words.

LAVIE

INBAC

NUBERK

CAUABS

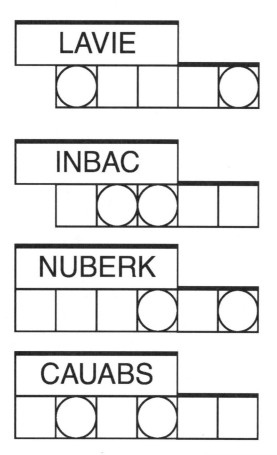

O.K. Dad

Don't ride them
too hard

HOW THE RANCH
KIDS RODE THEIR
HORSES ON
A HOT DAY.

Now arrange the circled letters to form the
surprise answer, as suggested by the above
cartoon.

Print answer here

JUMBLE®

Unscramble these four Jumbles, one letter to each square, to form four ordinary words.

LAQUI

LUGBY

THELLA

KOUNOH

This should draw a crowd

YE OLDE BAR

WHEN THE BAR OWNER INSTALLED A SIGN, IT BECAME A ---

Now arrange the circled letters to form the surprise answer, as suggested by the above cartoon.

Print answer here "◯◯◯◯ ◯◯◯"

JUMBLE®

Unscramble these four Jumbles, one letter to each square, to form four ordinary words.

SARBS

NICEW

PLAICH

LIMWED

May I help you?

He's one of the best

NECESSARY IN AUTOMOBILE CIRCLES.

Now arrange the circled letters to form the surprise answer, as suggested by the above cartoon.

Print answer here

JUMBLE®

Unscramble these four Jumbles, one letter to
each square, to form four ordinary words.

STRYT

YORRS

LAUMSY

RUMIAD

They don't have
a prenuptial
agreement

WHEN HE WED
THE RICH WIDOW,
HE DIDN'T ---

Now arrange the circled letters to form the
surprise answer, as suggested by the above
cartoon.

*Print answer
here*

JUMBLE®

Unscramble these four Jumbles, one letter to
each square, to form four ordinary words.

CURCO

LEEXI

LAASSI

DIMPOU

Oh, no!
What do I
do now?

WHEN THE AGING
BEAUTY QUEEN
DEVELOPED LAUGH
LINES, IT WAS---

Now arrange the circled letters to form the
surprise answer, as suggested by the above
cartoon.

Print answer here

JUMBLE

Unscramble these four Jumbles, one letter to
each square, to form four ordinary words.

ALVAN

ULARR

NEBATE

GEPLED

She made
her own
dress

WHEN THE SEAM-
STRESS GOT
MARRIED, HER
LIFE WAS ---

Now arrange the circled letters to form the
surprise answer, as suggested by the above
cartoon.

Print answer here " ◯◯◯◯◯◯◯ "

JUMBLE®

Unscramble these four Jumbles, one letter to each square, to form four ordinary words.

YOHNP

URUGA

TEANIN

SLEENT

Ahem

THIS CAN BE DROPPED WHEN MANNERS ARE BOORISH.

Now arrange the circled letters to form the surprise answer, as suggested by the above cartoon.

Print answer here A ⬭⬭⬭⬭⬭⬭ ⬭⬭⬭⬭

JUMBLE®

Unscramble these four Jumbles, one letter to
each square, to form four ordinary words.

NYMAG

THOUY

RECHOM

TINBAD

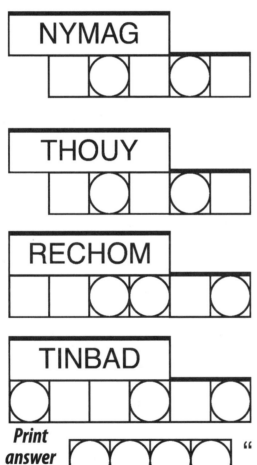

The winners
get the cake

It's outta
here

THE BAKER PLAYED
IN THE PICNIC BASE-
BALL GAME BECAUSE
HE MADE A ...

Now arrange the circled letters to form the
surprise answer, as suggested by the above
cartoon.

**Print
answer
here**

" "

JUMBLE®

Unscramble these four Jumbles, one letter to each square, to form four ordinary words.

LIVIG

BYRIN

LARIUT

GRACIT

Where were you on the night of...?

Rare, medium or...?

THE TRIAL LAWYER LIKED TO BARBEQUE BECAUSE HE ENJOYED ...

Now arrange the circled letters to form the surprise answer, as suggested by the above cartoon.

Print answer here

JUMBLE®

Unscramble these four Jumbles, one letter to
each square, to form four ordinary words.

NAALC

SHAWS

DARZAH

PLIDIM

Can you help me?
I need a new jib

See him

BOB

WHAT THE
YACHTSMAN
SOUGHT IN THE
BOAT SHOP.

Now arrange the circled letters to form the
surprise answer, as suggested by the above
cartoon.

*Print answer
here*   A "〇〇〇〇〇" 〇〇〇

JUMBLE®

Unscramble these four Jumbles, one letter to each square, to form four ordinary words.

IRATT

BROEP

TUCLED

NIMPED

Welcome to Chez Cement

EATING LUNCH ON A SIDEWALK CAN DO THIS.

Now arrange the circled letters to form the surprise answer, as suggested by the above cartoon.

Print answer here

" ⬡⬡⬡⬡ " AN ⬡⬡⬡⬡⬡⬡⬡⬡⬡

JUMBLE®

Unscramble these four Jumbles, one letter to
each square, to form four ordinary words.

BYBEA

ULIPP

DRAHLY

HARTOU

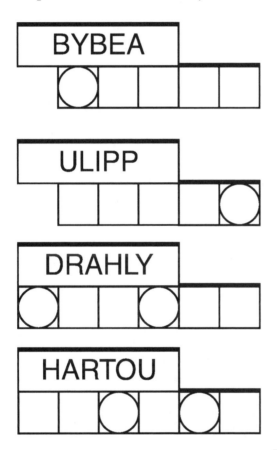

Not very stylish

THE MILLINERY SHOP
LOST SALES BECAUSE
THE MERCHANDISE
WAS ...

Now arrange the circled letters to form the
surprise answer, as suggested by the above
cartoon.

Print answer here

73

JUMBLE®

Unscramble these four Jumbles, one letter to
each square, to form four ordinary words.

VEDEL

CAGIM

MADENT

HIENAL

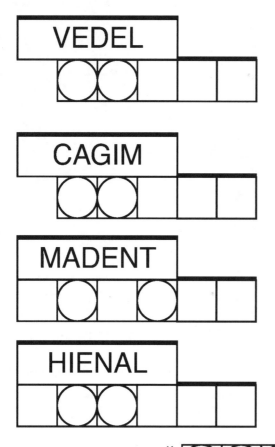

He's a natural

DESPITE THE LATEST
TRAINING EQUIPMENT,
THE BOXER'S PUNCHES
WERE ...

Now arrange the circled letters to form the
surprise answer, as suggested by the above
cartoon.

Print answer here " ⬡⬡⬡⬡ " ⬡⬡⬡⬡

JUMBLE®

Unscramble these four Jumbles, one letter to
each square, to form four ordinary words.

DYNAS

TWAHR

HELBIT

YERTAW

How bright do
you want it?

WHAT DAD HAD TO
KNOW WHEN HE
CHANGED THE
LIGHT BULB.

Now arrange the circled letters to form the
surprise answer, as suggested by the above
cartoon.

Print answer here

75

JUMBLE®

Unscramble these four Jumbles, one letter to
each square, to form four ordinary words.

OSHUE

ROHTT

REVAEB

LESING

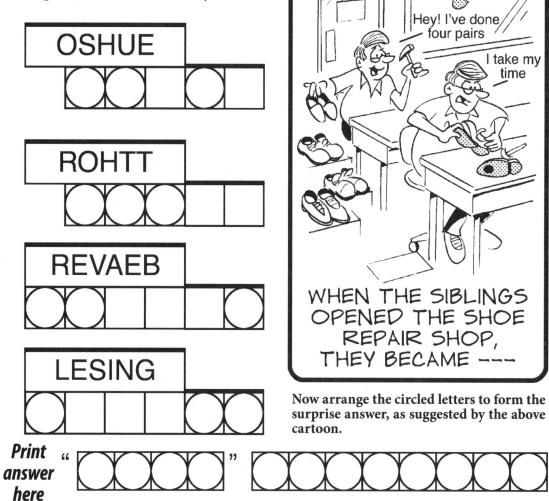

Hey! I've done
four pairs

I take my
time

WHEN THE SIBLINGS
OPENED THE SHOE
REPAIR SHOP,
THEY BECAME ---

Now arrange the circled letters to form the
surprise answer, as suggested by the above
cartoon.

Print
answer
here

" ⬭⬭⬭⬭ " ⬭⬭⬭⬭⬭⬭⬭⬭⬭

JUMBLE®

Unscramble these four Jumbles, one letter to
each square, to form four ordinary words.

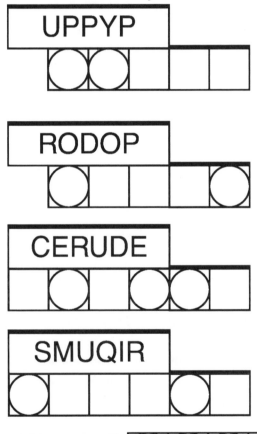

UPPYP

RODOP

CERUDE

SMUQIR

The trees are
loaded and I'm off

You look nice

WHEN THE CHRISTMAS
TREE GROWER WENT
TO MARKET, HE ---

Now arrange the circled letters to form the
surprise answer, as suggested by the above
cartoon.

Print answer
here " ◯◯◯◯◯◯◯ " ◯◯

JUMBLE ®

Unscramble these four Jumbles, one letter to each square, to form four ordinary words.

WOLLY

UCLID

ENIAMA

SNOOPI

The street is flooding

WHAT THE RAIN DOES WHEN IT KEEPS UP.

Now arrange the circled letters to form the surprise answer, as suggested by the above cartoon.

Print answer here

JUMBLE®

Unscramble these four Jumbles, one letter to each square, to form four ordinary words.

INGEF

VIPTO

RIMOAH

LAYREY

Check the newspaper or go online

WHAT THE DEADBEAT LOOKED FOR WHEN HIS GIRL TOLD HIM TO GET A JOB.

Now arrange the circled letters to form the surprise answer, as suggested by the above cartoon.

Print answer here

JUMBLE®

Unscramble these four Jumbles, one letter to each square, to form four ordinary words.

THABE

DUNBO

CLOPIE

TRYFOS

Can I have $20?

WHAT IT TAKES TO MAKE DAD A SOFT TOUCH.

Now arrange the circled letters to form the surprise answer, as suggested by the above cartoon.

Print answer here A ⬡⬡⬡⬡ ⬡⬡⬡⬡⬡

JUMBLE®

Unscramble these four Jumbles, one letter to each square, to form four ordinary words.

ADGUY

TROFY

BIEMIB

LEVVET

WHAT THE DRUMMER DROVE TO THE PARTY.

Now arrange the circled letters to form the surprise answer, as suggested by the above cartoon.

Print answer here A " ⬡⬡⬡⬡⬡⬡ "

JUMBLE®

Unscramble these four Jumbles, one letter to each square, to form four ordinary words.

FHASE

DRIOF

ALOONG

KOOCIE

This is the best. No traffic jam. No parking worries

WHAT HE APPRECIATED WHEN HE TOOK THE SUBWAY.

Now arrange the circled letters to form the surprise answer, as suggested by the above cartoon.

Print answer here THE " ◯◯◯◯ " ◯◯◯◯

JUMBLE®

Unscramble these four Jumbles, one letter to each square, to form four ordinary words.

NOUCE

TALEV

ATJECK

REDAIM

Another homer. He's great   He'll go to the big club in no time

OFTEN FOUND
IN A MINOR
LEAGUE BALLPARK.

Now arrange the circled letters to form the surprise answer, as suggested by the above cartoon.

Print answer here

" ◯◯◯◯◯ " ◯◯◯◯◯◯

JUMBLE®

Unscramble these four Jumbles, one letter to each square, to form four ordinary words.

BRILO

YEAPE

YOLDUC

BOAMEA

BZZZZZZ

Check all the rooms

It's probably just the battery

WHEN THE SMOKE DETECTOR WENT OFF IN THE WEE HOURS, THEY WERE ---

Now arrange the circled letters to form the surprise answer, as suggested by the above cartoon.

Print answer here " ◯◯◯◯◯◯◯ "

84

JUMBLE®

Unscramble these four Jumbles, one letter to each square, to form four ordinary words.

DYNOS

DAUTI

HARTEG

THALIG

I oil weekly and check the cord

WHAT HE MAINTAINED WHEN HE WAS IN CHARGE OF THE FLAGPOLE.

Now arrange the circled letters to form the surprise answer, as suggested by the above cartoon.

Print answer here A ⬡⬡⬡⬡ " ⬡⬡⬡⬡⬡⬡⬡⬡⬡ "

JUMBLE®

Unscramble these four Jumbles, one letter to
each square, to form four ordinary words.

DYPUG

JOUMB

YOJECK

TEXMEP

You're on
your own,
son

HOW THE PARENTS
WANTED TO KEEP
THE COLLEGE GRAD'S
ROOM.

Now arrange the circled letters to form the
surprise answer, as suggested by the above
cartoon.

Print answer here

JUMBLE®

Unscramble these four Jumbles, one letter to each square, to form four ordinary words.

NALST

GINOG

COZADI

TROBEH

That should keep the flu away

I didn't feel a thing

Get Vaccinated today!

WHAT THE HUNTER SAID WHEN HE WAS INOCULATED.

Now arrange the circled letters to form the surprise answer, as suggested by the above cartoon.

Print answer here ⟨◯◯◯◯ " ◯◯◯◯ "⟩

JUMBLE®

Unscramble these four Jumbles, one letter to
each square, to form four ordinary words.

LEREB

TEAGA

DETHOB

LARTEY

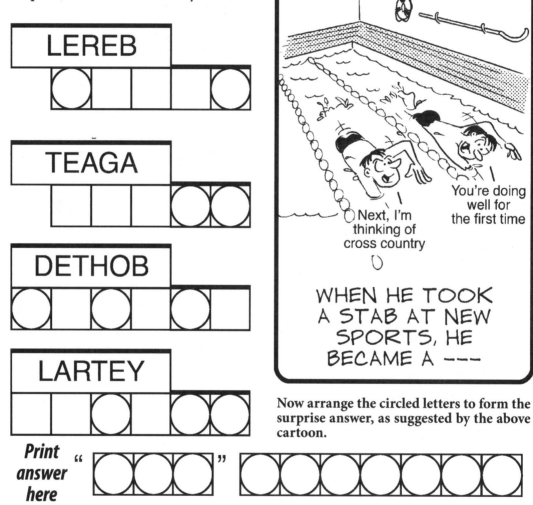

You're doing
well for
the first time

Next, I'm
thinking of
cross country

WHEN HE TOOK
A STAB AT NEW
SPORTS, HE
BECAME A ---

Now arrange the circled letters to form the
surprise answer, as suggested by the above
cartoon.

Print
answer
here   " ◯◯◯ "   ◯◯◯◯◯◯◯◯

JUMBLE®

Unscramble these four Jumbles, one letter to each square, to form four ordinary words.

LARNG

INBAR

CLAUNY

MOOSER

!!@?!
Just when I'm on a deadline

PRESS

WHEN HIS CURSOR FAILED, THE REPORTER BECAME A ----

Now arrange the circled letters to form the surprise answer, as suggested by the above cartoon.

Print answer here

89

JUMBLE®

Unscramble these four Jumbles, one letter to
each square, to form four ordinary words.

DAHYN

HALTE

KRUTEY

PARMEE

I need this in
an hour

I was meeting
my wife
for dinner

WHAT THE LAST—
MINUTE FITTING DID
TO THE TAILOR'S
EVENING PLANS.

Now arrange the circled letters to form the
surprise answer, as suggested by the above
cartoon.

*Print
answer
here*

"⃝⃝⃝⃝⃝⃝⃝" ⃝⃝⃝⃝

90

JUMBLE®

Unscramble these four Jumbles, one letter to each square, to form four ordinary words.

KANCK

SHOCA

MEDOCY

WEGNIT

Yes, sir.
Whatever you
say, sir

You don't
deserve
a raise

NEVER TALK TURKEY
WITH YOUR BOSS
WHEN YOU ARE ---

Now arrange the circled letters to form the surprise answer, as suggested by the above cartoon.

Print answer here

JUMBLE®

Unscramble these four Jumbles, one letter to
each square, to form four ordinary words.

VOARS

CUEJI

LANITE

HERTHS

I'll see you in court

WHEN SHE DUMPED
HER FILTHY RICH
HUSBAND, SHE TOOK
HIM TO ---

Now arrange the circled letters to form the
surprise answer, as suggested by the above
cartoon.

Print answer here

JUMBLE®

Unscramble these four Jumbles, one letter to
each square, to form four ordinary words.

REEMY

USOED

LAUBBE

CANNUE

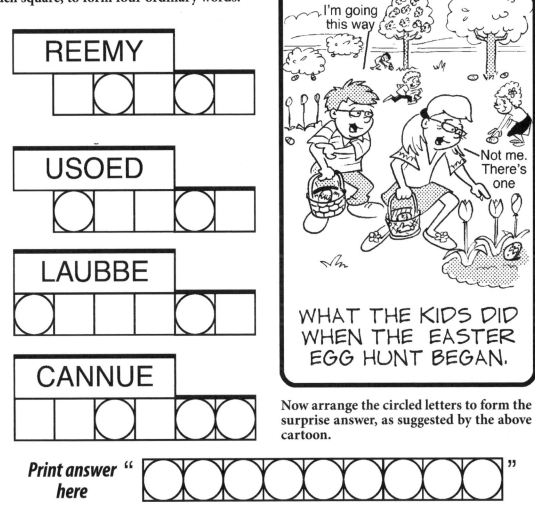

I'm going
this way

Not me.
There's
one

WHAT THE KIDS DID
WHEN THE EASTER
EGG HUNT BEGAN.

Now arrange the circled letters to form the
surprise answer, as suggested by the above
cartoon.

Print answer "
here

JUMBLE®

Unscramble these four Jumbles, one letter to each square, to form four ordinary words.

ROUCS

YURMM

SINOUF

GRATTE

No more eating out

WHAT THE DAIRY FARMER FACED WHEN MILK PRICES TUMBLED.

Now arrange the circled letters to form the surprise answer, as suggested by the above cartoon.

Print answer here A ◯◯◯◯ ◯◯◯◯◯◯◯

JUMBLE®

Unscramble these four Jumbles, one letter to
each square, to form four ordinary words.

EPPIR

SOLEO

REFERT

ELEVAN

Oh, dear, I feel another
rhyme coming on!

WHEN THE AILING
POET TOOK TO
HIS BED, HE ---

Now arrange the circled letters to form the
surprise answer, as suggested by the above
cartoon.

**Print answer
here**

" "

JUMBLE®

Unscramble these four Jumbles, one letter to
each square, to form four ordinary words.

MASCK

NOKTE

YEMMAH

SCAFAR

The winners get $10,000

PAY TO
THE ORDER OF: TEAM TIPPIE
TEN THOUSAND $$ $10,000

WHEN THE CHESS
TEAM WON, THEY
BECAME ---

Now arrange the circled letters to form the
surprise answer, as suggested by the above
cartoon.

Print answer
here   " ⬡⬡⬡⬡⬡ "   ⬡⬡⬡⬡⬡

JUMBLE®

Unscramble these four Jumbles, one letter to each square, to form four ordinary words.

YAGIL

WEJEL

DOONBY

LOWELY

The pasta is almost done

Not now

WHAT HIS WIFE DID WHEN THE GAME WENT INTO OVERTIME.

Now arrange the circled letters to form the surprise answer, as suggested by the above cartoon.

Print answer here " ⬡⬡⬡⬡⬡⬡ "

JUMBLE®

Unscramble these four Jumbles, one letter to each square, to form four ordinary words.

UFYSS

TREEB

WORMAR

PEBSIC

It was fair and balanced

Your story was slanted

FAVORED BY THE REPORTER, BUT NOT BY THE DRY CLEANER.

Now arrange the circled letters to form the surprise answer, as suggested by the above cartoon.

Print answer here A ⬡⬡⬡⬡⬡ " ⬡⬡⬡⬡⬡⬡ "

98

JUMBLE®

Unscramble these four Jumbles, one letter to each square, to form four ordinary words.

BLAYM

WILLT

VACTAR

CHISPY

Let's call it a day

WHAT THE DIRECTOR SAID WHEN THE MUMMY SCENE WAS SHOT.

Now arrange the circled letters to form the surprise answer, as suggested by the above cartoon.

Print answer here ⬭⬭ ' ⬭ A " ⬭⬭⬭⬭ "

JUMBLE®

Unscramble these four Jumbles, one letter to
each square, to form four ordinary words.

LEVOG

REVUC

YASUNE

HARKEW

He had two
big offers

Cheap at
any price

THE CONDUCTOR
NEGOTIATED A
LUCRATIVE CONTRACT
BECAUSE HE - - -

Now arrange the circled letters to form the
surprise answer, as suggested by the above
cartoon.

Print
answer
here

⬡⬡⬡⬡ THE " ⬡⬡⬡⬡⬡ "

JUMBLE®

Unscramble these four Jumbles, one letter to each square, to form four ordinary words.

TAROA

FIMOT

PATUCE

FITHES

We need invitations, flowers, bridesmaids and groomsmen.

WHAT IT TAKES TO GET MARRIED.

Now arrange the circled letters to form the surprise answer, as suggested by the above cartoon.

Print answer here

THE "⬭⬭⬭⬭" ⬭⬭⬭⬭⬭

JUMBLE®

Unscramble these four Jumbles, one letter to each square, to form four ordinary words.

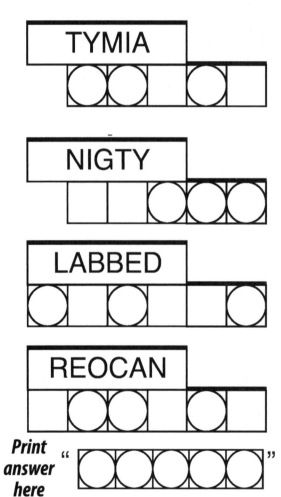

TYMIA

NIGTY

LABBED

REOCAN

Print answer here " ◯◯◯◯◯ "

Just like our stock price, up and down

WHEN THE CORPORATE DIRECTORS WENT SURFING, THEY HAD A ---

Now arrange the circled letters to form the surprise answer, as suggested by the above cartoon.

◯◯◯◯◯◯◯

JUMBLE®

Unscramble these four Jumbles, one letter to
each square, to form four ordinary words.

GANET

ZYIZD

UNTRAB

AGMANE

Turn that
down!

HOW THE TEEN'S
LOUD MUSIC
LEFT DAD.

Now arrange the circled letters to form the
surprise answer, as suggested by the above
cartoon.

Print answer
here " ◯◯◯ - ◯◯◯◯◯◯ "

JUMBLE®

Unscramble these four Jumbles, one letter to each square, to form four ordinary words.

DRUFA

MYPUB

PERUSH

NUTJAY

Is he available?
He looks married

WHAT A SINGLE GIRL SHOULDN'T LOOK FOR WHEN SHE'S LOOKING FOR THIS

Now arrange the circled letters to form the surprise answer, as suggested by the above cartoon.

Print answer here A

JUMBLE®

Unscramble these four Jumbles, one letter to
each square, to form four ordinary words.

NOOZE

KLUFE

FUITTO

FORPIT

SALE

You look
10 years
younger

WHEN HE BOUGHT A
HAIRPIECE FOR HIS
BALD HEAD,
HE HAD ---

Now arrange the circled letters to form the
surprise answer, as suggested by the above
cartoon.

**Print answer
here**

IT

JUMBLE®

Unscramble these four Jumbles, one letter to each square, to form four ordinary words.

RUETT

KNACS

RICCAT

HAPUNC

A DOCTOR DOES THIS ON THE GOLF RANGE OR IN HIS OFFICE.

Now arrange the circled letters to form the surprise answer, as suggested by the above cartoon.

Print answer here

106

JUMBLE®

Unscramble these four Jumbles, one letter to each square, to form four ordinary words.

PLEEX

GOLIO

PRUMAK

GONNIG

Ma'am, your credit card

HUDSON'S

WHEN THE ARCH-AEOLOGIST BOUGHT A WRINKLE-FREE WARD-ROBE, SHE LEFT ---

Now arrange the circled letters to form the surprise answer, as suggested by the above cartoon.

Print answer here THE " ⬭⬭⬭⬭⬭ " ⬭⬭⬭

107

JUMBLE®

Unscramble these four Jumbles, one letter to each square, to form four ordinary words.

KEDAB

HAABS

YALAWY

TRUBET

No problem

WHAT THE LAID-BACK PICKPOCKET LIKED TO DO.

Now arrange the circled letters to form the surprise answer, as suggested by the above cartoon.

Print answer here ⬡⬡⬡⬡⬡ IT " ⬡⬡⬡⬡ "

JUMBLE®

Unscramble these four Jumbles, one letter to
each square, to form four ordinary words.

TOBAL

INSIF

RELUSY

UNTEAB

Right this way,
Mrs. Van Snoot

You're not
on the list

THEY GUARDED THE
ENTRANCE TO THE
POSH CLUB, BECAUSE
THEY KNEW THE ---

Now arrange the circled letters to form the
surprise answer, as suggested by the above
cartoon.

Print answer
here "◯◯◯" AND "◯◯◯◯"

JUMBLE®

Unscramble these four Jumbles, one letter to
each square, to form four ordinary words.

RIBBE

JARAH

CLUDED

BIHRDY

Bessie's leading them home

CLANG CLANG

I ♥ JUMBLE

WHAT THE FARMER
DID WHEN THE COWS
CAME HOME FOR
MILKING.

Now arrange the circled letters to form the
surprise answer, as suggested by the above
cartoon.

**Print answer
here** ⬡⬡⬡⬡⬡ THE ⬡⬡⬡⬡

110

JUMBLE®

Unscramble these four Jumbles, one letter to each square, to form four ordinary words.

MYLOD

MUPLE

CORRAN

DOBCIE

I'm coughing and sneezing

EVEN ROYALTY HAS TO PUT UP WITH THIS.

Now arrange the circled letters to form the surprise answer, as suggested by the above cartoon.

Print answer here

A " ⃝⃝⃝⃝⃝⃝ " ⃝⃝⃝⃝

JUMBLE

Unscramble these four Jumbles, one letter to
each square, to form four ordinary words.

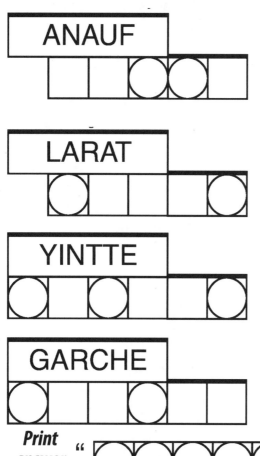

ANAUF

LARAT

YINTTE

GARCHE

HE BECAME A ROADIE
FOR THE ROCK
BAND BECAUSE HE
COULD ---

Now arrange the circled letters to form the
surprise answer, as suggested by the above
cartoon.

Print
answer
here

" ◯◯◯◯◯ " A ◯◯◯◯

JUMBLE®

Unscramble these four Jumbles, one letter to each square, to form four ordinary words.

NUKKS

BYLUR

DROOVE

THROOC

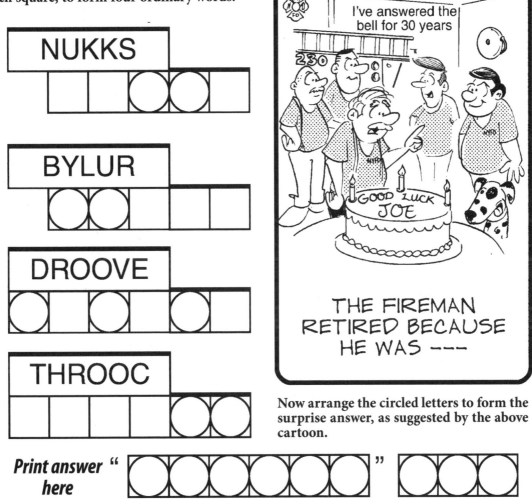

I've answered the bell for 30 years

GOOD LUCK JOE

THE FIREMAN RETIRED BECAUSE HE WAS ----

Now arrange the circled letters to form the surprise answer, as suggested by the above cartoon.

Print answer here " ⬡⬡⬡⬡⬡⬡ " ⬡⬡⬡

113

JUMBLE

Unscramble these four Jumbles, one letter to
each square, to form four ordinary words.

EJYTT

BAWLY

INJOAD

NUMMIE

WHEN THE DOOR
GOT STUCK, IT
WAS A ---

Now arrange the circled letters to form the
surprise answer, as suggested by the above
cartoon.

Print answer here

JUMBLE®

Unscramble these four Jumbles, one letter to
each square, to form four ordinary words.

GUAVE

LOVEC

CLAGEN

SIHARD

Shall we
open another
bottle of wine?

DRINKING OR
EATING TOO MUCH
CAN GET YOU A ---

Now arrange the circled letters to form the
surprise answer, as suggested by the above
cartoon.

Print answer here

JUMBLE®

Unscramble these four Jumbles, one letter to each square, to form four ordinary words.

BICUT

NISOB

SEJERY

EKATIN

I'm tired of castles, churches and water

AFTER VIEWING MANY SIGHTS ON THEIR 2-WEEK CRUISE, THEY WERE ---

Now arrange the circled letters to form the surprise answer, as suggested by the above cartoon.

Print answer here "◯◯◯" ◯◯◯◯

JUMBLE®

Unscramble these four Jumbles, one letter to each square, to form four ordinary words.

YICIL

IMNEC

LARVEM

TALOZE

Too warm and too flat

A STATE BACHELOR SKIERS AVOID.

Now arrange the circled letters to form the surprise answer, as suggested by the above cartoon.

Print answer here

JUMBLE®

Unscramble these four Jumbles, one letter to each square, to form four ordinary words.

FELCT

LORGY

CINORI

BIDITT

LOANS
DEPT.

You're quite a
success story

WHAT THE BANKER
GAVE THE SELF-MADE
MILLIONAIRE.

Now arrange the circled letters to form the surprise answer, as suggested by the above cartoon.

Print answer here A ⬡⬡⬡ OF ⬡⬡⬡⬡⬡⬡

JUMBLE®

Unscramble these four Jumbles, one letter to each square, to form four ordinary words.

PEDYT

GUNDE

NYLARX

SNUIGE

but I thought...

Hey, not that one!

WHEN THE LUMBER-JACK CUT DOWN THE WRONG TREE, IT WAS AN ---

Now arrange the circled letters to form the surprise answer, as suggested by the above cartoon.

Print answer here " ◯◯ - ◯◯◯◯◯ "

JUMBLE®

Unscramble these four Jumbles, one letter to
each square, to form four ordinary words.

ALZEH

SLEBS

DABALL

UNTTAR

WHEN THE
ASTRONAUTS WERE
LAUNCHED INTO
ORBIT, THEY ---

Now arrange the circled letters to form the
surprise answer, as suggested by the above
cartoon.

***Print answer
here*** ◯◯◯ A " ◯◯◯◯◯ "

JUMBLE®

Unscramble these four Jumbles, one letter to each square, to form four ordinary words.

ELLIS

TIBUL

NEPAHP

HACING

I'm being swept off my feet

There he goes again

THE PARTYGOER THOUGHT IT WAS GOOD FOR A LAUGH, BUT IT WAS ---

Now arrange the circled letters to form the surprise answer, as suggested by the above cartoon.

Print answer here

JUMBLE®

Unscramble these four Jumbles, one letter to
each square, to form four ordinary words.

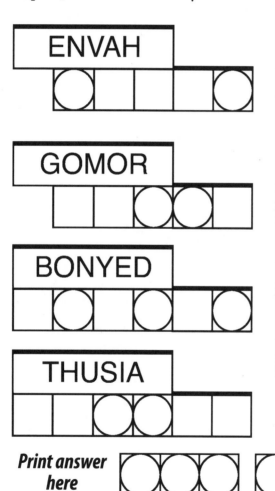

ENVAH

GOMOR

BONYED

THUSIA

I'm sick
tomorrow

WHAT THE EMPLOYEES
DID WHEN THE BOSS
WENT ON VACATION.

Now arrange the circled letters to form the
surprise answer, as suggested by the above
cartoon.

Print answer here

JUMBLE

Unscramble these four Jumbles, one letter to
each square, to form four ordinary words.

KALOC

IGNAT

TRYAGE

BOEDUL

HE NEVER GOT
AROUND TO
MARRYING,
BUT HE ---

Now arrange the circled letters to form the
surprise answer, as suggested by the above
cartoon.

Print answer here

JUMBLE.

Unscramble these four Jumbles, one letter to
each square, to form four ordinary words.

UNESE

NOPLY

SOACLE

MIEPED

He wrote a
long note

WHEN THE AUTHOR
ESCAPED FROM
PRISON, THE WARDEN
SAID IT WAS A ---

Now arrange the circled letters to form the
surprise answer, as suggested by the above
cartoon.

Print answer here ◯◯◯◯ OF THE " ◯◯◯ "

124

JUMBLE®

Unscramble these four Jumbles, one letter to each square, to form four ordinary words.

BUMIE

UNGTS

INTYME

YALDED

I'm going to stay here for two weeks

But we've only got a three-day pass

THE SOLDIER DIDN'T RETURN TO BASE BECAUSE HE WAS----

Now arrange the circled letters to form the surprise answer, as suggested by the above cartoon.

Print answer here " ⃝⃝⃝⃝⃝⃝ " ⃝⃝⃝⃝⃝⃝

JUMBLE.

Unscramble these four Jumbles, one letter to
each square, to form four ordinary words.

CEHKT

HUDCY

OSANTA

GLUCED

How can I stop fumbling?

WHAT THE RUNNING
BACK CALLED THE
TEAM PSYCHIATRIST.

Now arrange the circled letters to form the
surprise answer, as suggested by the above
cartoon.

Print
answer THE "⬭⬭⬭⬭" ⬭⬭⬭⬭⬭
here

JUMBLE®

Unscramble these four Jumbles, one letter to each square, to form four ordinary words.

FELKA

TRAFC

RITHEM

LUDGEE

All he thinks about is numbers

THE ACCOUNTANT SEEMED UNIMPORTANT WHEN HE WAS DESCRIBED AS ---

Now arrange the circled letters to form the surprise answer, as suggested by the above cartoon.

Print answer here

A " ◯◯◯◯◯◯ - ◯◯◯◯ "

JUMBLE®

Unscramble these four Jumbles, one letter to each square, to form four ordinary words.

YIPTE

DARUG

LISHEC

HUDOLS

What are you humming?

WHAT THE LIVELY HAIRDRESSER LIKED TO DO.

Now arrange the circled letters to form the surprise answer, as suggested by the above cartoon.

Print answer here

◯◯◯◯ ◯◯ AND ◯◯◯

JUMBLE®

Unscramble these four Jumbles, one letter to each square, to form four ordinary words.

HOBUG

NLFAK

GAUHTT

MUSCLY

C'mon, let's dance

This is not for me

WHY THE SECRETARY LEFT THE OFFICE PARTY.

Now arrange the circled letters to form the surprise answer, as suggested by the above cartoon.

Print answer here   SHE WAS "⬭⬭⬭⬭⬭" ⬭⬭⬭⬭

JUMBLE®

Unscramble these four Jumbles, one letter to
each square, to form four ordinary words.

HEANN

KOSTE

THACAT

AIRLAD

C'mon!

WHAT MOST
BASEBALL BRAWLS
TURN INTO.

Now arrange the circled letters to form the
surprise answer, as suggested by the above
cartoon.

Print answer here A ⬚⬚ - ⬚⬚⬚⬚⬚⬚⬚

JUMBLE®

Unscramble these four Jumbles, one letter to
each square, to form four ordinary words.

NAPAG

ANBLK

INMALY

GAZZIG

I do all the
work. When
are you...

WHEN HIS WIFE KEPT
HARPING ON HIS LAZY
WAYS, HE HAD A----

Now arrange the circled letters to form the
surprise answer, as suggested by the above
cartoon.

**Print
answer
here**   " ⬡⬡⬡⬡⬡⬡⬡ " ⬡⬡⬡⬡

131

JUMBLE®

Unscramble these four Jumbles, one letter to
each square, to form four ordinary words.

CYDER

YARDT

DACROW

LOSFIS

How are you
holding up?

WHEN THE DRIVER
MADE A PIT
STOP, HE ---

Now arrange the circled letters to form the
surprise answer, as suggested by the above
cartoon.

Print answer here ◯◯◯ " ◯◯◯◯◯ "

JUMBLE®

Unscramble these four Jumbles, one letter to
each square, to form four ordinary words.

JEDDA

EGUSS

HINCLE

TENNIV

Let's take
a break

HE THOUGHT HE
WAS LIGHT ON HIS
FEET, BUT ---

Now arrange the circled letters to form the
surprise answer, as suggested by the above
cartoon.

Print answer here

JUMBLE®

Unscramble these four Jumbles, one letter to
each square, to form four ordinary words.

LEVVA

ULIQT

MALORF

GELISH

...then the flower girl
and finally the
bride

HOW THE PLANNER
EXPLAINED THE
WEDDING REHEARSAL.

Now arrange the circled letters to form the
surprise answer, as suggested by the above
cartoon.

Print
answer AN
here

JUMBLE®

Unscramble these four Jumbles, one letter to
each square, to form four ordinary words.

THIRM

SMIPK

CHORCT

NURPEY

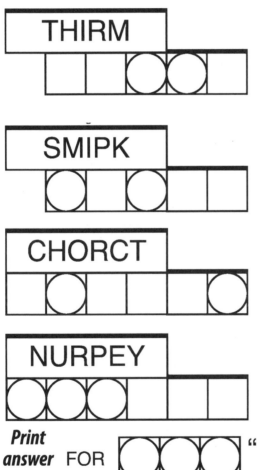

I was at a
costume
ball

ONE-HOUR
SERVICE

2 FOR 1

WHY THE
"FAIRY PRINCESS"
WENT TO THE
PHOTO STORE.

Now arrange the circled letters to form the
surprise answer, as suggested by the above
cartoon.

*Print
answer
here* FOR " "

JUMBLE®

Unscramble these four Jumbles, one letter to each square, to form four ordinary words.

SEPOI

YAPOS

RALCOR

RHODIA

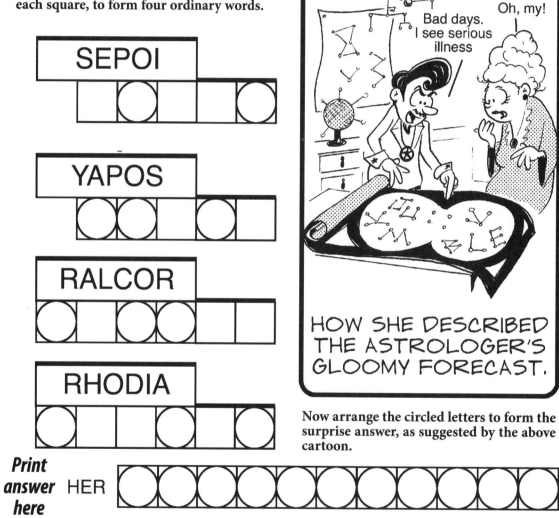

Bad days. I see serious illness

Oh, my!

HOW SHE DESCRIBED THE ASTROLOGER'S GLOOMY FORECAST.

Now arrange the circled letters to form the surprise answer, as suggested by the above cartoon.

Print answer here

HER

JUMBLE®

Unscramble these four Jumbles, one letter to
each square, to form four ordinary words.

GARBE

HOVUC

DOYLEM

VERROF

I'm out in the
fresh air
all day

Dave's Dogs

WHY HE TRADED HIS
HOT DOG STAND
FOR A PUSH CART.

Now arrange the circled letters to form the
surprise answer, as suggested by the above
cartoon.

Print answer here NO ◯◯◯◯-◯◯◯◯

137

JUMBLE®

Unscramble these four Jumbles, one letter to
each square, to form four ordinary words.

NOJIT

LAGOW

CHUNQE

NORSEP

Hello.
Is anybody there?

WHEN THE CELL PHONE
USER WAS PUT ON
HOLD ON A CROWDED
BUS, HE WAS ---

Now arrange the circled letters to form the
surprise answer, as suggested by the above
cartoon.

Print answer
here   A " ⬡⬡⬡⬡⬡⬡ " ⬡⬡

JUMBLE®

Unscramble these four Jumbles, one letter to each square, to form four ordinary words.

BASUQ

LUNCE

STOFFE

SLAVAS

The grass is thirsty

FOR SOME, "USE LESS" ADVICE DURING A WATER SHORTAGE IS ---

Now arrange the circled letters to form the surprise answer, as suggested by the above cartoon.

Print answer here

JUMBLE®

Unscramble these four Jumbles, one letter to each square, to form four ordinary words.

OTTOH

YASAS

LOVVEE

RIVFEY

It's $750 a month.
Here's the key

5A

WHAT THE POSTMAN
WAS GIVEN WHEN HE
RENTED THE
APARTMENT.

Now arrange the circled letters to form the surprise answer, as suggested by the above cartoon.

Print answer here A " ◯◯◯◯ " ◯◯◯◯

JUMBLE®

Unscramble these four Jumbles, one letter to
each square, to form four ordinary words.

BIRAB

IBARR

FLOAFY

KEGATS

Make sure all
the doors are
locked

I'll check the
windows, too

FEARS CAN
LEAD TO THIS.

Now arrange the circled letters to form the
surprise answer, as suggested by the above
cartoon.

Print answer here

JUMBLE®

Unscramble these four Jumbles, one letter to each square, to form four ordinary words.

SYLOU

UGLID

PYNTEL

UNPOOC

Shhhh!

Look at those pants

I would never...

THE GOLFER LEFT THE LIBRARY BECAUSE HIS SLACKS WERE---

Now arrange the circled letters to form the surprise answer, as suggested by the above cartoon.

Print answer here

JUMBLE®

Unscramble these four Jumbles, one letter to
each square, to form four ordinary words.

TRINP

RODUG

WROFUR

INDATE

The current was
too strong

We'll pull
you off

WHAT THE SUBMARINE
FACED WHEN IT RAN
INTO TROUBLE.

Now arrange the circled letters to form the
surprise answer, as suggested by the above
cartoon.

*Print answer
here* AN " ☐☐☐☐☐☐ " ☐☐☐

JUMBLE®

Unscramble these four Jumbles, one letter to
each square, to form four ordinary words.

AXTEC

KYACT

DROICH

TAXHOR

WHAT THE BALL-
PLAYER AND THE
FISHERMAN HAD IN
COMMON.

Now arrange the circled letters to form the
surprise answer, as suggested by the above
cartoon.

Print
answer
here
THE ⬡⬡⬡⬡⬡ OF ⬡⬡⬡ ⬡⬡⬡

JUMBLE®

Unscramble these four Jumbles, one letter to
each square, to form four ordinary words.

KOCHE

ENFLO

EXGONY

ZIFLEZ

Now they can
enjoy their food
without swatting

WHAT THE PILOTS
CREATED WHEN THEY
SPRAYED THE
PICNIC AREA.

Now arrange the circled letters to form the
surprise answer, as suggested by the above
cartoon.

**Print
answer
here**   A   " ◯◯-◯◯◯ " ◯◯◯◯

JUMBLE®

Unscramble these four Jumbles, one letter to each square, to form four ordinary words.

VOFAR

MAFLE

POWNEA

SIDURA

I guess I should have studied

WHAT THE LAZY STUDENT SAID WHEN HE FLUNKED THE SPELLING TEST.

Now arrange the circled letters to form the surprise answer, as suggested by the above cartoon.

Print answer here

JUMBLE®

Unscramble these four Jumbles, one letter to
each square, to form four ordinary words.

AMGUT

HAKSY

WALCOL

PANICT

Another round of
belt tightening

WHY HE NEEDED A
BANDAGE WHEN HE
GOT HIS
WEEKLY CHECK.

Now arrange the circled letters to form the
surprise answer, as suggested by the above
cartoon.

Print answer here HIS ◯◯◯ ◯◯◯ ◯◯◯

JUMBLE®

Unscramble these four Jumbles, one letter to each square, to form four ordinary words.

FLATA

DARIC

GUBORE

GEENER

WHAT THE MEDICAL STUDENTS CONSIDERED THE LECTURE ON BODY PARTS.

Now arrange the circled letters to form the surprise answer, as suggested by the above cartoon.

Print answer here AN ☐☐☐☐☐ ☐☐☐☐☐☐☐

JUMBLE®

Unscramble these four Jumbles, one letter to
each square, to form four ordinary words.

ESTAC

SQUET

CLIPES

CUDINT

Bob, will give
you trims today

A GOOD THING
TO DO IN
BARBER SCHOOL.

Now arrange the circled letters to form the
surprise answer, as suggested by the above
cartoon.

Print answer here " ⬡⬡⬡ " ⬡⬡⬡⬡⬡

149

JUMBLE®

Unscramble these four Jumbles, one letter to each square, to form four ordinary words.

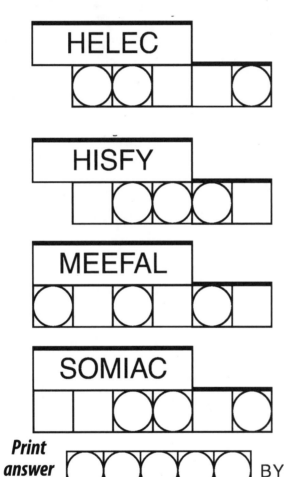

HELEC

HISFY

MEEFAL

SOMIAC

Nothing matches

Why I never ...

WHEN HE WORE THE LOUD OUTFIT, THE PARTYGOERS SAID HE WAS IN A ---

Now arrange the circled letters to form the surprise answer, as suggested by the above cartoon.

Print answer here ⬡⬡⬡⬡⬡ BY ⬡⬡⬡⬡⬡⬡⬡

JUMBLE®

Unscramble these four Jumbles, one letter to each square, to form four ordinary words.

EUQUE

DEPIT

FACTUE

BANCOR

I think he'll like this one NECKWEAR

WHAT SHE BOUGHT FOR HER BOYFRIEND.

Now arrange the circled letters to form the surprise answer, as suggested by the above cartoon.

Print answer here   A " ◯◯◯◯ " ◯◯◯

JUMBLE

Unscramble these four Jumbles, one letter to
each square, to form four ordinary words.

CUFOS

UNYTT

WOINDS

WHEPEN

These tricks
are hard

PLAYING WITH A
YO-YO HAS ITS ---

Now arrange the circled letters to form the
surprise answer, as suggested by the above
cartoon.

Print answer here ⬡⬡⬡ AND ⬡⬡⬡⬡⬡

JUMBLE®

Unscramble these four Jumbles, one letter to each square, to form four ordinary words.

GITUL

GOUCH

DIMFOY

BLAURT

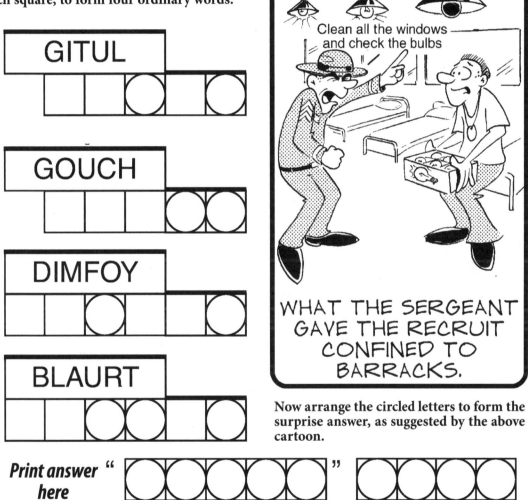

Clean all the windows and check the bulbs

WHAT THE SERGEANT GAVE THE RECRUIT CONFINED TO BARRACKS.

Now arrange the circled letters to form the surprise answer, as suggested by the above cartoon.

Print answer here " ◯◯◯◯◯ " ◯◯◯◯

153

JUMBLE

Unscramble these four Jumbles, one letter to
each square, to form four ordinary words.

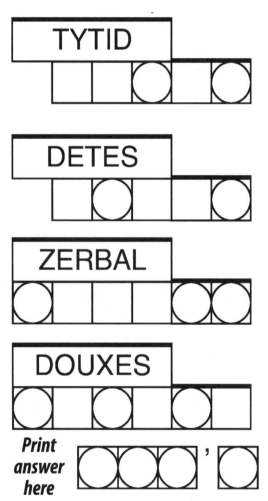

TYTID

DETES

ZERBAL

DOUXES

WHAT HIS
DOMINEERING
BRIDE SAID AT THE
WEDDING CEREMONY.

Now arrange the circled letters to form the
surprise answer, as suggested by the above
cartoon.

Print answer here ◯◯◯ ' ◯ ◯◯◯◯◯◯◯

JUMBLE®

Unscramble these four Jumbles, one letter to
each square, to form four ordinary words.

DRAUF

PENIT

SCULIE

KAUMPE

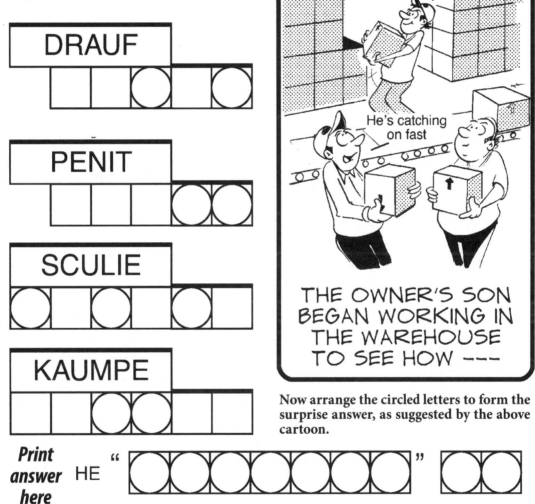

He's catching
on fast

THE OWNER'S SON
BEGAN WORKING IN
THE WAREHOUSE
TO SEE HOW ---

Now arrange the circled letters to form the
surprise answer, as suggested by the above
cartoon.

Print
answer   HE   "⃝⃝⃝⃝⃝⃝⃝⃝" ⃝⃝
here

JUMBLE®

Unscramble these four Jumbles, one letter to
each square, to form four ordinary words.

BYMUP

MIRGY

STABEK

EGMAIP

WHAT THE PURSE
SALE TURNED INTO.

Now arrange the circled letters to form the
surprise answer, as suggested by the above
cartoon.

Print answer here   A " ⬡⬡⬡⬡ " ⬡⬡⬡

JUMBLE®

Unscramble these four Jumbles, one letter to each square, to form four ordinary words.

ENTAK

DARAW

DILVER

STEJAM

There's a 30% discount today

I'll take two

WHEN HE BOUGHT A BOX OF CANDY, IT TURNED INTO A---

Now arrange the circled letters to form the surprise answer, as suggested by the above cartoon.

Print answer here " ⭘⭘⭘⭘⭘ " ⭘⭘⭘⭘

157

JUMBLE®

Unscramble these four Jumbles, one letter to each square, to form four ordinary words.

MEPIR

ROAPE

WHALLO

RATTAR

I'll put a pretty bow on it

WHAT THE CLERK LISTENED TO WHILE SHE WORKED.

Now arrange the circled letters to form the surprise answer, as suggested by the above cartoon.

Print answer here ⭕⭕⭕⭕ ⭕⭕⭕

JUMBLE®

Unscramble these four Jumbles, one letter to each square, to form four ordinary words.

YARRA

CINEW

PROPHE

UNTAUM

Your shiny head is blinding me

That's enough!

ONE TOO MANY
JOKES ABOUT
BALDING
CAN DO THIS.

Now arrange the circled letters to form the surprise answer, as suggested by the above cartoon.

Print answer here " "

JUMBLE®

Unscramble these four Jumbles, one letter to each square, to form four ordinary words.

CONOR

REQUE

TINISS

LIFTLE

I find you guilty.

WHAT THE
JUDGE'S RULING
AMOUNTED TO.

Now arrange the circled letters to form the surprise answer, as suggested by the above cartoon.

Print answer here A " ⬡⬡⬡⬡⬡⬡⬡⬡ "

JUMBLE®

Unscramble these four Jumbles, one letter to each square, to form four ordinary words.

INNEL

TACCH

VANGER

DISPUT

JEFF, MICHAEL, DINNER!

You can hear her a mile away

WHAT MOM USED TO CALL THE BOYS HOME FOR DINNER.

Now arrange the circled letters to form the surprise answer, as suggested by the above cartoon.

Print answer here

JUMBLE®

Unscramble these four Jumbles, one letter to
each square, to form four ordinary words.

VIILC

RYSAC

GHARNA

RESEGY

THE PATIENT LEFT
THE DENTIST
BECAUSE HE GOT ‒‒‒

Now arrange the circled letters to form the
surprise answer, as suggested by the above
cartoon.

Print answer here ON ◯◯◯ ◯◯◯◯◯◯

JUMBLE®

SAFARI

Challenger Puzzles

JUMBLE®

Unscramble these six Jumbles, one letter to each square, to form six ordinary words.

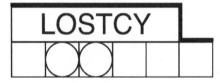

LOSTCY

SPOLGE

MAROFT

POMSIE

GURDIT

RUJINO

Hey, you really dented my door

A CARELESS DRIVER CAN LEAVE THIS.

Now arrange the circled letters to form the surprise answer, as suggested by the above cartoon.

Print answer here

A ⬭⬭⬭⬭ "⬭⬭⬭⬭⬭⬭⬭⬭⬭⬭"

JUMBLE®

Unscramble these six Jumbles, one letter to each square, to form six ordinary words.

MNADAM

CIRION

CATATH

RATHEH

DAGPOA

SIDEME

Not one button out of place

MAINTAINED BY THE HONOR GUARD WHEN THE FLAG WAS RAISED.

Now arrange the circled letters to form the surprise answer, as suggested by the above cartoon.

Print answer here

A ◯◯◯◯ " ◯◯◯◯◯◯◯◯ "

JUMBLE®

Unscramble these six Jumbles, one letter to each square, to form six ordinary words.

THAGUT

BURPAT

FLOUJY

NOMOAR

LUMUTT

KATINE

First loop it over and then under

WHAT THE BOY SCOUT SOLVED TO EARN HIS MERIT BADGE.

Now arrange the circled letters to form the surprise answer, as suggested by the above cartoon.

Print answer here

A " ⬡⬡⬡⬡⬡⬡ " ⬡⬡⬡⬡⬡⬡⬡

166

JUMBLE®

Unscramble these six Jumbles, one letter to each square, to form six ordinary words.

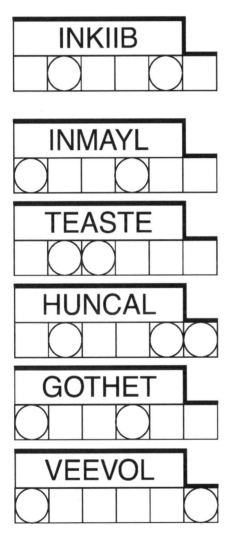

INKIIB

INMAYL

TEASTE

HUNCAL

GOTHET

VEEVOL

WHEN THEY FOUND EACH OTHER AT CHOIR PRACTICE, IT WAS---

Now arrange the circled letters to form the surprise answer, as suggested by the above cartoon.

Print answer here

A " ⬡⬡⬡⬡⬡⬡ " ⬡⬡⬡⬡⬡⬡⬡⬡

JUMBLE®

Unscramble these six Jumbles, one letter to
each square, to form six ordinary words.

DIBOUT

NOPHTY

SYTRUT

SWACHE

CILTIA

GOHMEA

WHAT AN EATING
CONTEST CAN BE.

Now arrange the circled letters to form the
surprise answer, as suggested by the above
cartoon.

Print answer here

JUMBLE®

Unscramble these six Jumbles, one letter to each square, to form six ordinary words.

SMALID

NAPOWE

FEWURC

BIEFLE

FRIMAF

LORFIC

Bon Voyage

You're sailing into jail

WHAT THE AUTHORITIES GAVE THE CRUISE SHIP STOWAWAY

Now arrange the circled letters to form the surprise answer, as suggested by the above cartoon.

Print answer here

AN " ◯◯◯◯◯◯◯◯ " ◯◯◯◯-◯◯◯

JUMBLE®

Unscramble these six Jumbles, one letter to
each square, to form six ordinary words.

HABINS

CLOWAL

DRIMBO

GETURT

STAFIE

ERAUSS

Done!
Move out soldier,
NEXT!

HOW THE ARMY
BARBER MET HIS
DAILY QUOTA

Now arrange the circled letters to form the
surprise answer, as suggested by the above
cartoon.

Print answer here

HE ⟨ ⟩⟨ ⟩⟨ ⟩⟨ ⟩ " ⟨ ⟩⟨ ⟩⟨ ⟩⟨ ⟩⟨ ⟩ ⟨ ⟩⟨ ⟩⟨ ⟩⟨ ⟩ "

170

JUMBLE®

Unscramble these six Jumbles, one letter to each square, to form six ordinary words.

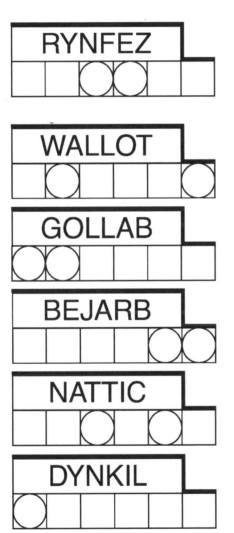

RYNFEZ

WALLOT

GOLLAB

BEJARB

NATTIC

DYNKIL

You cut me off!

You cut me off!

WHEN THE GEOMETRY TEACHER'S ROAD RAGE LED TO A CRASH, IT TURNED INTO A ---

Now arrange the circled letters to form the surprise answer, as suggested by the above cartoon.

Print answer here

" ◯◯◯◯◯ - ◯◯◯◯◯◯ "

JUMBLE®

Unscramble these six Jumbles, one letter to each square, to form six ordinary words.

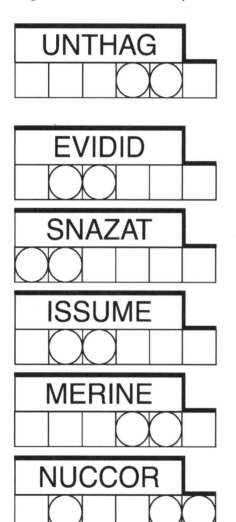

UNTHAG

EVIDID

SNAZAT

ISSUME

MERINE

NUCCOR

The flu is going around

COUGH
COUGH
ACHOO

WHEN MANY PEOPLE ARE ADMITTED TO HOSPITALS.

Now arrange the circled letters to form the surprise answer, as suggested by the above cartoon.

Print answer here

172

JUMBLE®

Unscramble these six Jumbles, one letter to each square, to form six ordinary words.

UNROAD

VALBER

FEEGUR

METROH

LEGALY

SWEDIT

I don't believe your excuses

SHE BROKE UP WITH THE MOUNTAIN CLIMBER BECAUSE HE WAS ...

Now arrange the circled letters to form the surprise answer, as suggested by the above cartoon.

Print answer here

◯◯◯◯◯◯◯ ON ◯◯◯ " ◯◯◯◯◯ "

JUMBLE®

Unscramble these six Jumbles, one letter to
each square, to form six ordinary words.

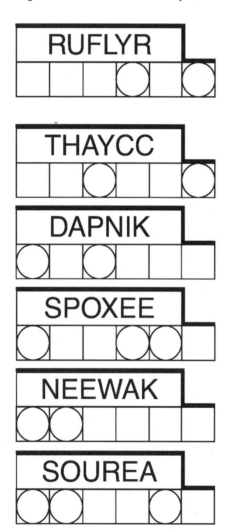

RUFLYR

THAYCC

DAPNIK

SPOXEE

NEEWAK

SOUREA

I'm on
it, boss

Your report
is due

IN

WHAT TOMORROW
WILL BRING FOR
A PROCRASTINATOR.

Now arrange the circled letters to form the
surprise answer, as suggested by the above
cartoon.

Print answer here

JUMBLE®

Unscramble these six Jumbles, one letter to each square, to form six ordinary words.

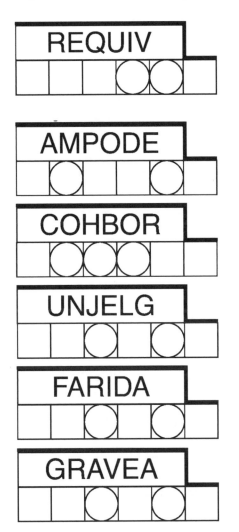

REQUIV

AMPODE

COHBOR

UNJELG

FARIDA

GRAVEA

My last delivery of the day

WHAT THE
MESSENGER
USED TO
GET AROUND.

Now arrange the circled letters to form the surprise answer, as suggested by the above cartoon.

Print answer here

A

JUMBLE®

Unscramble these six Jumbles, one letter to each square, to form six ordinary words.

SINOVI

FRAITY

TOBENN

PREDIM

YLKGNI

GLUTLE

HONEST BOB'S

Lots of miles left on this one

LIKE NEW

THE COUPLE SAVED FOR A RAINY DAY BY AVOIDING THIS.

Now arrange the circled letters to form the surprise answer, as suggested by the above cartoon.

Print answer here

◯◯◯◯◯◯◯ " ◯◯◯◯◯◯ "

JUMBLE®

Unscramble these six Jumbles, one letter to each square, to form six ordinary words.

COLOTE

INLOVI

CARILA

DHINER

BAYTER

GELIGG

If he's not here in two minutes, the wedding's off

WHEN THE GROOM WAS LATE, THE BRIDE MADE A---

Now arrange the circled letters to form the surprise answer, as suggested by the above cartoon.

Print answer here

" ◯◯◯◯◯◯ " ◯◯◯◯◯◯

JUMBLE®

Unscramble these six Jumbles, one letter to each square, to form six ordinary words.

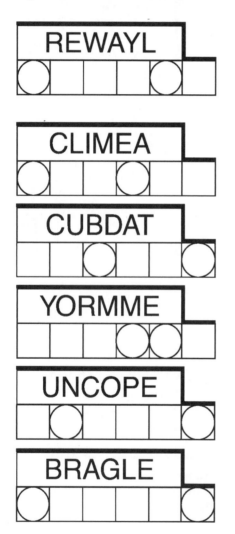

REWAYL

CLIMEA

CUBDAT

YORMME

UNCOPE

BRAGLE

Look at him jump

This is fun

WHEN THE FISHERMAN HOOKED THE SAILFISH, HE HAD A ---

Now arrange the circled letters to form the surprise answer, as suggested by the above cartoon.

Print answer here

178

JUMBLE®

Unscramble these six Jumbles, one letter to each square, to form six ordinary words.

LARMIN

DAMTLE

JOLTES

GOOSTE

DABBIE

EXLUDE

We'll have another round

WHEN THE CONTORTIONISTS VISITED A COUPLE OF BARS, THEY WERE ---

Now arrange the circled letters to form the surprise answer, as suggested by the above cartoon.

Print answer here

( ) ( ) ( ) ( ) ( ) " ( ) ( ) ( ) ( ) ( ) ( ) ( ) "

JUMBLE®

Unscramble these six Jumbles, one letter to
each square, to form six ordinary words.

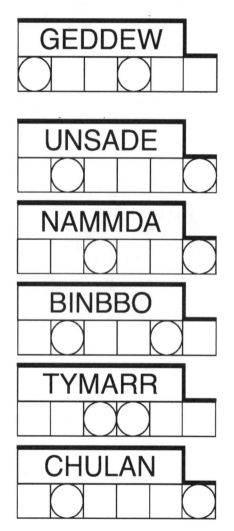

GEDDEW

UNSADE

NAMMDA

BINBBO

TYMARR

CHULAN

He holds the world record

I'm thirsty. Get me some water, NOW!

WHAT THE OLYMPIC
STAR LIKED
TO THROW.

Now arrange the circled letters to form the
surprise answer, as suggested by the above
cartoon.

Print answer here

HIS " ⬡⬡⬡⬡⬡⬡ " ⬡⬡⬡⬡⬡⬡

JUMBLE®

Unscramble these six Jumbles, one letter to each square, to form six ordinary words.

YARRIT

DOBUTI

ORDINO

INMOOT

PASCUM

EEDCAC

He hung it up last year

THE RETIRED CEO ENJOYED BEING THIS.

Now arrange the circled letters to form the surprise answer, as suggested by the above cartoon.

Print answer here

" ⬡⬡⬡⬡⬡ " OF ⬡⬡⬡⬡⬡⬡⬡⬡⬡

JUMBLE®

Unscramble these six Jumbles, one letter to each square, to form six ordinary words.

SMURTE

GOUHNE

PRYNTA

RIMMOE

GINMOH

FLUTAR

...and a horse in every barn

I've heard that before

WHEN THE COWBOYS LISTENED TO THE POLITICIAN, THEY SAID HE ---

Now arrange the circled letters to form the surprise answer, as suggested by the above cartoon.

Print answer here

JUMBLE®

Unscramble these six Jumbles, one letter to each square, to form six ordinary words.

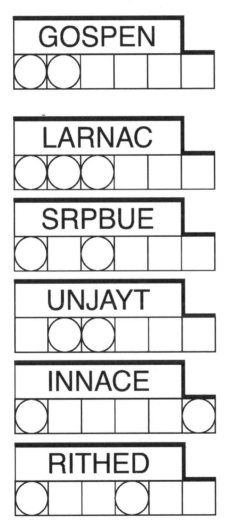

GOSPEN

LARNAC

SRPBUE

UNJAYT

INNACE

RITHED

$2 to clean your windshield, ma'am

WHAT THE TEENS DID AFTER THE ICE STORM.

Now arrange the circled letters to form the surprise answer, as suggested by the above cartoon.

Print answer here

"⬡⬡⬡⬡⬡⬡⬡" ⬡⬡ ⬡⬡⬡⬡

Answers

1. **Jumbles:** BLOAT EAGLE THRIVE UNLOCK
   Answer: When the dentist and his manicurist wife fought, it was — TOOTH AND NAIL

2. **Jumbles:** CHICK QUOTA ECZEMA BECOME
   Answer: What the boomerang champion sought when he lost the contest — A "COMEBACK"

3. **Jumbles:** BOGUS CLEFT HELIUM PHYSIC
   Answer: What it takes to spot a distant ice site — EYE SIGHT

4. **Jumbles:** FUDGE MURKY WINNOW JERSEY
   Answer: The first thing the teen took when he got his driver's license — A "JOY" RIDE

5. **Jumbles:** BUILT ALTAR HUNTER OVERDO
   Answer: When the wheel was invented, it created a — REVOLUTION

6. **Jumbles:** IDIOM AUDIT GRASSY TETHER
   Answer: When the city slicker tried milking a cow, the result was — AN "UDDER" MESS

7. **Jumbles:** DRAWL GRAIN POORLY WORTHY
   Answer: A tickets mix-up can result in a — ROW ROW

8. **Jumbles:** SKUNK FEWER MUFFIN TURTLE
   Answer: He was named taxidermist of the year because he — KNEW HIS "STUFF"

9. **Jumbles:** NOISY AHEAD UPTOWN BAZAAR
   Answer: What a cookbook author will do — EAT HIS WORDS

10. **Jumbles:** ICILY BRAND BUTANE MUFFLE
    Answer: What it takes to ship a package cross country — A "BUNDLE"

11. **Jumbles:** MAIZE CHANT ADROIT FINITE
    Answer: What he paid when he hired the tax advisor — ATTENTION

12. **Jumbles:** MOUNT ANISE HANSOM SMUDGE
    Answer: What the male model received when he posed in the suit — A "HANDSOME" SUM

13. **Jumbles:** CUBIT CRANK GROUCH FORAGE
    Answer: What he drove when he bought a used car — A TOUGH BARGAIN

14. **Jumbles:** MOUSY DOWNY MUSLIN PENMAN
    Answer: What it cost the London mogul to lose some pounds — SOME POUNDS

15. **Jumbles:** VAGUE TYPED URCHIN MARVEL
    Answer: What the surgeon turned into at the annual party — A REAL CUT UP

16. **Jumbles:** LEAFY THINK HITHER PASTRY
    Answer: What happened when he got the bill for the roof? — HE HIT THE "RAFTERS"

17. **Jumbles:** MINER BAGGY GUITAR UPHELD
    Answer: What the couple got in the lighting store — A "BRIGHT" IDEA

18. **Jumbles:** MINCE ALIAS NIMBLE SHANTY
    Answer: The workers described the nasty tycoon as — A MAN OF "MEANS"

19. **Jumbles:** SILKY FUROR OCCULT PARADE
    Answer: What a boxer will fight for that a woman has — A PURSE

20. **Jumbles:** COUPE ELDER LARYNX DELUXE
    Answer: What the janitor did when he played poker — HE "CLEANED" UP

21. **Jumbles:** CIVIL CREEL GOATEE ALPACA
    Answer: When the skinny little convict gained weight in prison, he was — AT "LARGE"

22. **Jumbles:** MEALY RABBI DOUBLE CIPHER
    Answer: What the warden did when the crooked barber escaped — "COMBED" THE AREA

23. **Jumbles:** NUDGE BILGE FLORID DREDGE
    Answer: What the violinist enjoyed doing in the garden — "FIDDLING"

24. **Jumbles:** UTTER SQUAB TRUISM INDUCE
    Answer: When the cook drained the huge pot of pasta, it was — QUITE A "STRAIN"

25. **Jumbles:** VERVE BRIAR INVERT DURESS
    Answer: When the aspiring poet got an idea during the night, he went from — BED TO VERSE

26. **Jumbles:** GROUP BISON LAYOFF NATURE
    Answer: When they went to the shark movie, it was — ABOUT A "FIN"

27. **Jumbles:** TARDY BLAZE HARROW MALADY
    Answer: When the seer read their fortune, she — HAD A "BALL"

28. **Jumbles:** DECRY UNCLE MALTED NUMBER
    Answer: A beauty queen will make her entrance to — ENTRANCE

29. **Jumbles:** ASSAY GUEST DEADLY ARCTIC
    Answer: When the rain ruined her hairdo, she was — "DIS-TRESSED"

30. **Jumbles:** RUSTY POWER BIGAMY COMPEL
    Answer: When the runabout stalled, it turned into — A "WOE" BOAT

31. **Jumbles:** PRIME CRAFT SEPTIC OUTWIT
    Answer: She married a novelist because he was — MISTER "WRITE"

32. **Jumbles:** OWING GUILD POPLIN KIMONO
    Answer: The blue-eyed blonde led the bird watchers because she was — GOOD "LOOKING"

33. **Jumbles:** POISE QUEUE BYWORD VARIED
    Answer: This can ruin a relationship — "BRIDE" IDEAS

34. **Jumbles:** CHOKE LUNGE THORAX BUNION
    Answer: When the magician made his beautiful helper disappear, she was — NOTHING TO LOOK AT

35. **Jumbles:** FELON CREEK PREFER AVENUE
    Answer: What the feuding neighbors had on the Fourth of July — A "FLARE" UP

36. **Jumbles:** ENACT FLUTE EMBODY WHOLLY
    Answer: When the old-time telegraph operator sent his hourly message, it was — ON THE "DOT"

37. **Jumbles:** SOAPY PLUSH PUDDLE BLAZER
    Answer: Acceptable when renting a beach umbrella — A "SHADY" DEAL

38. **Jumbles:** PYLON GIVEN INFLUX DISOWN
    Answer: Done by a laborer when he gets the job — FILLS THE "OPENING"

39. **Jumbles:** COUGH COLIC TAWDRY LAVISH
    Answer: What the tycoon resorted to when his assets were frozen — COLD CASH

40. **Jumbles:** TULLE SCARF POROUS HANGAR
    Answer: What she got when the sugar daddy gave her his credit card — A "CHARGE" OUT OF IT

41. **Jumbles:** CROON TACKY FARINA BRUTAL
    Answer: This takes some study before a big purchase — A BANK ACCOUNT

42. **Jumbles:** MAUVE DEMON ENTICE AWEIGH
    Answer: When the banker shed his suit for sweats, he felt like a — "CHANGED" MAN

43. **Jumbles:** LIMBO WHEEL STUPID BEHOLD
    Answer: When their new house was completed, the couple was — BUILD BILLED

44. **Jumbles:** AWASH HEAVY DOMINO GRAVEN
    Answer: A deposit at the blood bank is a — GOOD WAY TO "SAVE"

45. **Jumbles:** TEPID SPURN CANNED ENOUGH
    Answer: What the dietitian did when the English patient lost weight — GAINED "POUNDS"

46. **Jumbles:** PIANO GUILT CANINE MYSELF
    Answer: This can make for a "genial" evening — GIN AND ALE

47. **Jumbles:** ABHOR IMBUE SAILOR INJECT
    Answer: The groomer brushed the show horse's hair because it was — HIS "MANE" JOB

48. **Jumbles:** DAUNT LEECH BELLOW FEDORA
Answer: Too many square meals can make one —
WELL "ROUNDED"

49. **Jumbles:** COACH FEVER CORPSE TRIPLE
Answer: What the sheriff always has in a western movie —
A "STAR" ROLE

50. **Jumbles:** BELLE MAXIM PLACID VANITY
Answer: Even a king takes a back seat to this in a poker
game — AN ACE

51. **Jumbles:** PAGAN TOXIC BISECT FROTHY
Answer: How a night out on the town left him —
IN A "TIGHT" SPOT

52. **Jumbles:** POPPY SWOOP ROTATE TINGLE
Answer: What a photographer can do with a bored model —
GET "SNAPPY"

53. **Jumbles:** NOISE PANSY SYMBOL KETTLE
Answer: What it takes to become a ballroom dancer —
LOTS OF "STEPS"

54. **Jumbles:** MANLY LEGAL ELIXIR ICEBOX
Answer: When the manager let off steam, he was —
"BOILING"

55. **Jumbles:** BANDY ELITE FEMALE ACTUAL
Answer: It doesn't exist at the equator — LATITUDE

56. **Jumbles:** TRIPE GAUZE PSYCHE SCHEME
Answer: What the guard was between when he took a rest
— THE SHEETS

57. **Jumbles:** CROWN APART ENSIGN CASKET
Answer: The Hollywood astrologer liked to gossip because
she — KNEW THE "STARS"

58. **Jumbles:** MINOR FUNNY BEDECK JUMPER
Answer: What the soldiers did when they decided to get
married "JOINED" UP

59. **Jumbles:** DOWDY CHIDE NOZZLE TANGLE
Answer: When Mom scolded him for being lazy, Dad took
it — LYING DOWN

60. **Jumbles:** ALIVE CABIN BUNKER ABACUS
Answer: How the ranch kids rode their horses on a hot day
— BARE BACK

61. **Jumbles:** QUAIL BULGY LETHAL UNHOOK
Answer: When the bar owner installed a sign, it became a —
"HANG OUT"

62. **Jumbles:** BRASS WINCE CALIPH MILDEW
Answer: Necessary in automobile circles — WHEELS

63. **Jumbles:** TRYST SORRY ASYLUM RADIUM
Answer: When he wed the rich widow, he didn't —
MARRY AMISS

64. **Jumbles:** OCCUR EXILE ASSAIL PODIUM
Answer: When the aging beauty queen developed laugh
lines, it was — SERIOUS

65. **Jumbles:** NAVAL RURAL BEATEN PLEDGE
Answer: When the seamstress got married, her life was —
ALTARED

66. **Jumbles:** PHONY AUGUR INNATE NESTLE
Answer: This can be dropped when manners are boorish —
A STRONG HINT

67. **Jumbles:** MANGY YOUTH CHROME BANDIT
Answer: The baker played in the picnic baseball game
because he made a — GOOD "BATTER"

68. **Jumbles:** VIGIL BRINY RITUAL TRAGIC
Answer: The trial lawyer liked to barbeque because he
enjoyed — GRILLING

69. **Jumbles:** CANAL SWASH HAZARD LIMPID
Answer: What the yachtsman sought in the boat shop —
A "SAILS" MAN

70. **Jumbles:** TRAIT PROBE DULCET IMPEND
Answer: Eating lunch on the sidewalk can do this —
"CURB" AN APPETITE

71. **Jumbles:** ABBEY PUPIL HARDLY AUTHOR
Answer: The millinery shop lost sales because the
merchandise was — OLD HAT

72. **Jumbles:** DELVE MAGIC TANDEM INHALE
Answer: Despite the latest training equipment, the boxer's
punches were — "HAND" MADE

73. **Jumbles:** SANDY WRATH BLITHE WATERY
Answer: What Dad had to know when he changed the light
bulb — WHAT'S WATT

74. **Jumbles:** HOUSE TROTH BEAVER SINGLE
Answer: When the siblings opened the shoe repair shop,
they became — "SOLE" BROTHERS

75. **Jumbles:** PUPPY DROOP REDUCE SQUIRM
Answer: When the Christmas tree grower went to market,
he — "SPRUCED" UP

76. **Jumbles:** LOWLY LUCID ANEMIA POISON
Answer: What rain does when it keeps up — COMES DOWN

77. **Jumbles:** FEIGN PIVOT MOHAIR YEARLY
Answer: What the deadbeat looked for when his girl told him
to get a job — ANOTHER GIRL

78. **Jumbles:** BATHE BOUND POLICE FROSTY
Answer: What it takes to make Dad a soft touch —
A SOFT TOUCH

79. **Jumbles:** GAUDY FORTY IMBIBE VELVET
Answer: What the drummer drove to the party — A "BEATER"

80. **Jumbles:** SHEAF FIORD LAGOON COOKIE
Answer: What he appreciated when he took the subway —
THE "HOLE" RIDE

81. **Jumbles:** OUNCE VALET JACKET ADMIRE
Answer: Often found in a minor league ballpark —
"MAJOR" TALENT

82. **Jumbles:** BROIL PAYEE CLOUDY AMOEBA
Answer: When the smoke detector went off in the wee
hours, they were — "ALARMED"

83. **Jumbles:** SYNOD AUDIT GATHER ALIGHT
Answer: What he maintained when he was in charge of the
flagpole — A HIGH "STANDARD"

84. **Jumbles:** PUDGY JUMBO JOCKEY EXEMPT
Answer: How the parents wanted to keep the college grad's
room — EMPTY

85. **Jumbles:** SLANT GOING ZODIAC BOTHER
Answer: What the hunter said when he was inoculated —
GOOD "SHOT"

86. **Jumbles:** REBEL AGATE HOTBED REALTY
Answer: When he took a stab at new sports, he became a —
"TRY" ATHLETE

87. **Jumbles:** GNARL BRAIN LUNACY MOROSE
Answer: When his cursor failed, the reporter became a —
CURSER

88. **Jumbles:** HANDY LATHE TURKEY AMPERE
Answer: What the last-minute fitting did to the tailor's
evening plans — "ALTERED" THEM

89. **Jumbles:** KNACK CHAOS COMEDY TWINGE
Answer: Never talk turkey with your boss when you are —
CHICKEN

90. **Jumbles:** SAVOR JUICE ENTAIL THRESH
Answer: When she dumped her filthy rich husband, she took
him to — THE CLEANERS

91. **Jumbles:** EMERY DOUSE BAUBLE NUANCE
Answer: What the kids did when the Easter egg hunt began
— "SCRAMBLED"

92. **Jumbles:** SCOUR RUMMY FUSION TARGET
Answer: What the dairy farmer faced when milk prices
tumbled — A SOUR FUTURE

93. **Jumbles:** PIPER LOOSE FERRET LEAVEN
Answer: When the ailing poet took to his bed, he —
FELT "VERSE"

94. **Jumbles:** SMACK TOKEN MAYHEM FRACAS
Answer: When the chess team won, they became —
"CHECK" MATES

95. **Jumbles:** GAILY JEWEL NOBODY YELLOW
Answer: What his wife did when the game went into
overtime — "BOILED"

96. **Jumbles:** FUSSY BERET MARROW BICEPS
Answer: Favored by the reporter, but not the dry cleaner — A FREE "PRESS"

97. **Jumbles:** BALMY TWILL CRAVAT PHYSIC
Answer: What the director said when the mummy scene was shot — IT'S A "WRAP"

98. **Jumbles:** GLOVE CURVE UNEASY HAWKER
Answer: The conductor negotiated a lucrative contract because he — KNEW THE "SCORE"

99. **Jumbles:** AORTA MOTIF TEACUP FETISH
Answer: What it takes to get married — THE "RITE" STUFF

100. **Jumbles:** AMITY TYING DABBLE CORNEA
Answer: When the corporate directors went surfing, they had a — "BOARD" MEETING

101. **Jumbles:** AGENT DIZZY TURBAN MANAGE
Answer: How the teen's loud music left Dad — "EAR-ITATED"

102. **Jumbles:** FRAUD BUMPY PUSHER JAUNTY
Answer: What a single girl shouldn't look for when she's looking for this — A HUSBAND

103. **Jumbles:** OZONE FLUKE OUTFIT PROFIT
Answer: When he bought a hairpiece for his bald head, he had — TOUPEE FOR IT

104. **Jumbles:** UTTER SNACK ARCTIC PAUNCH
Answer: A doctor does this on the golf range or in his office — PRACTICES

105. **Jumbles:** EXPEL IGLOO MARKUP NOGGIN
Answer: When the archaeologist bought a wrinkle-free wardrobe, she left — THE "IRON" AGE

106. **Jumbles:** BAKED ABASH WAYLAY BUTTER
Answer: What the laid-back pickpocket liked to do — TAKE IT "EASY"

107. **Jumbles:** BLOAT FINIS SURELY BUTANE
Answer: They guarded the entrance to the posh club because they knew the — "INS" AND "OUTS"

108. **Jumbles:** BRIBE RAJAH CUDDLE HYBRID
Answer: What the farmer did when the cows came home for milking — HEARD THE HERD

109. **Jumbles:** MOLDY PLUME RANCOR BODICE
Answer: Even royalty has to put up with this — A "COMMON" COLD

110. **Jumbles:** FAUNA ALTAR ENTITY CHARGE
Answer: He became a roadie for the rock band because he could — "CARRY" A TUNE

111. **Jumbles:** SKUNK BURLY OVERDO COHORT
Answer: The fireman retired because he was — "BURNED" OUT

112. **Jumbles:** JETTY BYLAW ADJOIN IMMUNE
Answer: When the door got stuck, it was a — JAMB JAM

113. **Jumbles:** VAGUE CLOVE GLANCE RADISH
Answer: Drinking or eating too much can get you a — HANG OVER

114. **Jumbles:** CUBIT BISON JERSEY INTAKE
Answer: After viewing many sights on their 2-week cruise, they were — "SEE" SICK

115. **Jumbles:** ICILY MINCE MARVEL ZEALOT
Answer: A state bachelor skiers avoid — MATRIMONY

116. **Jumbles:** CLEFT GLORY IRONIC TIDBIT
Answer: What the banker gave the self-made millionaire — A LOT OF CREDIT

117. **Jumbles:** TYPED NUDGE LARYNX GENIUS
Answer: When the lumberjack cut down the wrong tree, it was an — "AX-IDENT"

118. **Jumbles:** HAZEL BLESS BALLAD TRUANT
Answer: When the astronauts were launched into orbit, they — HAD A "BLAST"

119. **Jumbles:** LISLE BUILT HAPPEN ACHING
Answer: The partygoer thought it was good for a laugh, but it was — LAUGHABLE

120. **Jumbles:** HAVEN GROOM BEYOND HIATUS
Answer: What the employees did when the boss went on vacation — HAD ONE TOO

121. **Jumbles:** CLOAK GIANT GYRATE DOUBLE
Answer: He never got around to marrying, but he — GOT AROUND

122. **Jumbles:** ENSUE PYLON SOLACE IMPEDE
Answer: When the author escaped from prison, the warden said it was a — SLIP OF THE "PEN"

123. **Jumbles:** IMBUE STUNG ENMITY DEADLY
Answer: The soldier didn't return to base because he was — "ABSENT" MINDED

124. **Jumbles:** KETCH DUCHY SONATA CUDGEL
Answer: What the running back called the team psychiatrist — THE "HEAD" COACH

125. **Jumbles:** FLAKE CRAFT HERMIT DELUGE
Answer: The accountant seemed unimportant when he was described as — A "FIGURE-HEAD"

126. **Jumbles:** PIETY GUARD CHISEL SHOULD
Answer: What the lively hairdresser liked to do — CURL UP AND DYE

127. **Jumbles:** BOUGH FLANK TAUGHT CLUMSY
Answer: Why the secretary left the office party — SHE WAS "BASH" FULL

128. **Jumbles:** HENNA STOKE ATTACH RADIAL
Answer: What most baseball brawls turn into — A NO-HITTER

129. **Jumbles:** PAGAN BLANK MAINLY ZIGZAG
Answer: When his wife kept harping on his lazy ways, he had a — "NAGGING" PAIN

130. **Jumbles:** DECRY TARDY COWARD FOSSIL
Answer: When the driver made a pit stop, he — WAS "TIRED"

131. **Jumbles:** JADED GUESS LICHEN INVENT
Answer: He thought he was light on his feet, but — SHE DIDN'T

132. **Jumbles:** VALVE QUILT FORMAL SLEIGH
Answer: How the planner explained the wedding rehearsal — AN AISLE TRIAL

133. **Jumbles:** MIRTH SKIMP CROTCH PENURY
Answer: Why the "fairy princess" went to the photo store — FOR HER "PRINTS"

134. **Jumbles:** POISE SOAPY CORRAL HAIRDO
Answer: How she described the astrologer's gloomy forecast — HER HORRORSCOPE

135. **Jumbles:** BARGE VOUCH MELODY FERVOR
Answer: Why he traded his hot dog stand for a push cart — NO OVER-HEAD

136. **Jumbles:** JOINT AGLOW QUENCH PERSON
Answer: When the cell phone user was put on hold on a crowded bus, he was — A "HANGER" ON

137. **Jumbles:** SQUAB UNCLE OFFSET VASSAL
Answer: For some, "use less" advice during a water shortage is — USELESS

138. **Jumbles:** TOOTH ASSAY EVOLVE VERIFY
Answer: What the postman was given when he rented the apartment — A "FLAT" RATE

139. **Jumbles:** RABBI BRIAR LAYOFF GASKET
Answer: Fears can lead to this — SAFER

140. **Jumbles:** LOUSY GUILD PLENTY COUPON
Answer: The golfer left the library because his slacks were — TOO LOUD

141. **Jumbles:** PRINT GOURD FURROW DETAIN
Answer: What the submarine faced when it ran into trouble — AN "UNDER" TOW

142. **Jumbles:** EXACT TACKY ORCHID THORAX
Answer: What the ballplayer and fisherman had in common — THE CATCH OF THE DAY

143. **Jumbles:** CHOKE FELON OXYGEN FIZZLE
Answer: What the pilots created when they sprayed the picnic area — A "NO-FLY" ZONE

144. **Jumbles:** FAVOR FLAME WEAPON RADIUS
Answer: What the lazy student said when he flunked the spelling test — WORDS FAIL ME

145. **Jumbles:** GAMUT SHAKY CALLOW CATNIP
Answer: Why he needed a bandage when he got his weekly check — HIS PAY WAS CUT

146. **Jumbles:** FATAL ACRID BROGUE RENEGE
Answer: What the medical students considered the lecture on body parts — AN ORGAN RECITAL

147. **Jumbles:** CASTE QUEST SPLICE INDUCT
Answer: A good thing to do in barber school — "CUT" CLASS

148. **Jumbles:** LEECH FISHY FEMALE MOSAIC
Answer: When he wore the loud outfit, the partygoers said he was in a — CLASH BY HIMSELF

149. **Jumbles:** QUEUE TEPID FAUCET CARBON
Answer: What she bought for her boyfriend — A "BEAU" TIE

150. **Jumbles:** FOCUS NUTTY DISOWN NEPHEW
Answer: Playing with a yo-yo has its — UPS AND DOWNS

151. **Jumbles:** GUILT COUGH MODIFY BRUTAL
Answer: What the sergeant gave the recruit confined to barracks — "LIGHT" DUTY

152. **Jumbles:** DITTY STEED BLAZER EXODUS
Answer: What his domineering bride said at the wedding ceremony — YOU'D BETTER

153. **Jumbles:** FRAUD INEPT SLUICE MAKEUP
Answer: The owner's son began working in the warehouse to see how — HE "STACKED" UP

154. **Jumbles:** BUMPY GRIMY BASKET MAGPIE
Answer: What the purse sale turned into — A "GRAB" BAG

155. **Jumbles:** TAKEN AWARD DRIVEL JETSAM
Answer: When he bought a box of candy, it turned into a — "SWEET" DEAL

156. **Jumbles:** PRIME OPERA HALLOW TARTAR
Answer: What the clerk listened to while she worked — WRAP RAP

157. **Jumbles:** ARRAY WINCE HOPPER AUTUMN
Answer: One too many jokes about balding can do this — WEAR "THIN"

158. **Jumbles:** CROON QUEER INSIST FILLET
Answer: What the judge's ruling amounted to — A "SENTENCE"

159. **Jumbles:** LINEN CATCH GRAVEN STUPID
Answer: What Mom used to call the boys home for dinner — LUNG DISTANCE

160. **Jumbles:** CIVIL SCARY HANGAR GEYSER
Answer: The patient left the dentist because he got — ON HIS NERVES

161. **Jumbles:** COSTLY GOSPEL FORMAT IMPOSE TURGID JUNIOR
Answer: A careless driver can leave this — A GOOD "IMPRESSION"

162. **Jumbles:** MADMAN IRONIC ATTACH HEARTH PAGODA DEMISE
Answer: Maintained by the honor guard when the flag was raised — A HIGH "STANDARD"

163. **Jumbles:** TAUGHT ABRUPT JOYFUL MAROON TUMULT INTAKE
Answer: What the boy scout solved to earn his merit badge — A "KNOTTY" PROBLEM

164. **Jumbles:** BIKINI MAINLY ESTATE LAUNCH GHETTO EVOLVE
Answer: When they found each other at choir practice, it was —A "CHANTS" MEETING

165: **Jumbles:** PYTHON TRUSTY CASHEW ITALIC HOMAGE
Answer: What an eating contest can be — TOUGH TO "STOMACH"

166. **Jumbles:** DISMAL WEAPON CURFEW BELIEF AFFIRM FROLIC
Answer: What the authorities gave the cruise ship stowaway — AN "OFFICIAL" SEND-OFF

167. **Jumbles:** BANISH CALLOW MORBID GUTTER FIESTA ASSURE
Answer: How the Army barber met his daily quota — HE USED "SHORT CUTS"

168. **Jumbles:** FRENZY TALLOW GLOBAL JABBER INTACT KINDLY
Answer: When the geometry teacher's road rage led to a crash, it turned into a — "WRECK-TANGLE"

169. **Jumbles:** NAUGHT DIVIDE STANZA MISUSE ERMINE CONCUR
Answer: When many people are admitted to hospitals — VISITING HOURS

170. **Jumbles:** AROUND VERBAL REFUGE MOTHER GALLEY WIDEST
Answer: She broke up with the mountain climber because he was — SELDOM ON THE "LEVEL"

171. **Jumbles:** FLURRY CATCHY KIDNAP EXPOSE WEAKEN AROUSE
Answer: What tomorrow will bring for a procrastinator — YESTERDAY'S WORK

172. **Jumbles:** QUIVER POMADE BROOCH JUNGLE AFRAID RAVAGE
Answer: What the messenger used to getaround — A REVOLVING DOOR

173. **Jumbles:** VISION RATIFY BONNET PRIMED KINGLY GULLET
Answer: The couple saved for a rainy day by avoiding this — GETTING "SOAKED"

174. **Jumbles:** OCELOT VIOLIN RACIAL HINDER BETRAY GIGGLE
Answer: When the groom was late, the bride made — "VEILED" THREAT

175. **Jumbles:** LAWYER MALICE ABDUCT MEMORY POUNCE GARBLE
Answer: When the fisherman hooked the sailfish, he had a — "REEL" GOOD TIME

176. **Jumbles:** MARLIN MALTED JOSTLE STOOGE BABIED DELUXE
Answer: When the contortionists visited a couple of bars, they were — DOUBLE "JOINTED"

177. **Jumbles:** WEDGED SUNDAE MADMAN BOBBIN MARTYR LAUNCH
Answer: What the Olympic star liked to throw — HIS "WEIGHT" AROUND

178. **Jumbles:** RARITY OUTBID INDOOR MOTION CAMPUS ACCEDE
Answer: The retired CEO enjoyed being this — "BORED" OF DIRECTORS

179. **Jumbles:** MUSTER ENOUGH PANTRY MEMOIR HOMING ARTFUL
Answer: When the cowboys listened to the politician, they said he — SHOT FROM THE LIP

180. **Jumbles:** SPONGE CARNAL SUPERB JAUNTY CANINE DITHER
Answer: What the teens did after the ice storm — "SCRAPED" UP CASH

Need More Jumbles®?

Jumble® Books

More than 175 puzzles each!

Jammin' Jumble®
$9.95 • ISBN: 1-57243-844-4

Java Jumble®
$9.95 • ISBN: 978-1-60078-415-6

Jazzy Jumble®
$9.95 • ISBN: 978-1-57243-962-7

Jet Set Jumble®
$9.95 • ISBN: 978-1-60078-353-1

Joyful Jumble®
$9.95 • ISBN: 978-1-60078-079-0

Juke Joint Jumble®
$9.95 • ISBN: 978-1-60078-295-4

Jumble® at Work
$9.95 • ISBN: 1-57243-147-4

Jumble® Celebration
$9.95 • ISBN: 978-1-60078-134-6

Jumble® Explosion
$9.95 • ISBN: 978-1-60078-078-3

Jumble® Fever
$9.95 • ISBN: 1-57243-593-3

Jumble® Fiesta
$9.95 • ISBN: 1-57243-626-3

Jumble® Fun
$9.95 • ISBN: 1-57243-379-5

Jumble® Galaxy
$9.95 • ISBN: 978-1-60078-583-2

Jumble® Genius
$9.95 • ISBN: 1-57243-896-7

Jumble® Getaway
$9.95 • ISBN: 978-1-60078-547-4

Jumble® Grab Bag
$9.95 • ISBN: 1-57243-273-X

Jumble® Jackpot
$9.95 • ISBN: 1-57243-897-5

Jumble® Jambalaya
$9.95 • ISBN: 978-1-60078-294-7

Jumble® Jamboree
$9.95 • ISBN: 1-57243-696-4

Jumble® Jitterbug
$9.95 • ISBN: 978-1-60078-584-9

Jumble® Jubilee
$9.95 • ISBN: 1-57243-231-4

Jumble® Juggernaut
$9.95 • ISBN: 978-1-60078-026-4

Jumble® Junction
$9.95 • ISBN: 1-57243-380-9

Jumble® Jungle
$9.95 • ISBN: 978-1-57243-961-0

Jumble® Madness
$9.95 • ISBN: 1-892049-24-4

Jumble® Mania
$9.95 • ISBN: 1-57243-697-2

Jumble® Safari
$9.95 • ISBN: 978-1-60078-675-4

Jumble® See & Search
$9.95 • ISBN: 1-57243-549-6

Jumble® See & Search 2
$9.95 • ISBN: 1-57243-734-0

Jumble® Sensation
$9.95 • ISBN: 978-1-60078-548-1

Jumble® Surprise
$9.95 • ISBN: 1-57243-320-5

Jumpin' Jumble®
$9.95 • ISBN: 978-1-60078-027-1

Outer Space Jumble®
$9.95 • ISBN: 978-1-60078-416-3

Rainy Day Jumble®
$9.95 • ISBN: 978-1-60078-352-4

Ready, Set, Jumble®
$9.95 • ISBN: 978-1-60078-133-0

Rock 'n' Roll Jumble®
$9.95 • ISBN: 978-1-60078-674-7

Sports Jumble®
$9.95 • ISBN: 1-57243-113-X

Summer Fun Jumble®
$9.95 • ISBN: 1-57243-114-8

Travel Jumble®
$9.95 • ISBN: 1-57243-198-9

TV Jumble®
$9.95 • ISBN: 1-57243-461-9

Oversize Jumble® Books

More than 500 puzzles each!

Generous Jumble®
$19.95 • ISBN: 1-57243-385-X

Giant Jumble®
$19.95 • ISBN: 1-57243-349-3

Gigantic Jumble®
$19.95 • ISBN: 1-57243-426-0

Jumbo Jumble®
$19.95 • ISBN: 1-57243-314-0

The Very Best of Jumble® BrainBusters
$19.95 • ISBN: 1-57243-845-2

Jumble® Crosswords™

More than 175 puzzles each!

More Jumble® Crosswords™
$9.95 • ISBN: 1-57243-386-8

Jumble® Crosswords™ Jackpot
$9.95 • ISBN: 1-57243-615-8

Jumble® Crosswords™ Jamboree
$9.95 • ISBN: 1-57243-787-1

Jumble® BrainBusters™

More than 175 puzzles each!

Jumble® BrainBusters™
$9.95 • ISBN: 1-892049-28-7

Jumble® BrainBusters™ II
$9.95 • ISBN: 1-57243-424-4

Jumble® BrainBusters™ III
$9.95 • ISBN: 1-57243-463-5

Jumble® BrainBusters™ IV
$9.95 • ISBN: 1-57243-489-9

Jumble® BrainBusters™ 5
$9.95 • ISBN: 1-57243-548-8

Jumble® BrainBusters™ Bonanza
$9.95 • ISBN: 1-57243-616-6

Boggle™ BrainBusters™
$9.95 • ISBN: 1-57243-592-5

Boggle™ BrainBusters™ 2
$9.95 • ISBN: 1-57243-788-X

Jumble® BrainBusters™ Junior
$9.95 • ISBN: 1-892049-29-5

Jumble® BrainBusters™ Junior II
$9.95 • ISBN: 1-57243-425-2

Fun in the Sun with Jumble® BrainBusters™
$9.95 • ISBN: 1-57243-733-2